EYEWITNESS
HORSE

Kulan

Woman and girl, wearing Spanish riding costumes, on dapple grey Andalusian

Bronze statuette of warrior on horseback, c. 550 BCE

Brass rowel spur, from South America, c. 1800

Henry VIII's full horse armour

Mule drawing Indian cart, c. 1840

Bronze plaque of warrior on horseback, from Benin in modern-day Nigeria, late 16th century

Foot and two side toes of *Anchitherium* fossil

Old shoe and nails removed from horse's hoof

EYEWITNESS
HORSE

Written by
Juliet Clutton-Brock

Mountain zebra

Shoeing a Shire horse

Dapple grey jumping

DK

Drum horse
and rider

Irish donkey pulling
cart, c.1850

DK | Penguin
Random
House

Project editor Marion Dent
Art editor Jutta Kaiser-Atcherley
Senior editor Helen Parker
Senior art editor Julia Harris
Production Louise Barratt
Picture research Diana Morris
Special photography Jerry Young, Karl Shone

RELAUNCH EDITION

DK UK

Senior editor Francesca Baines
Senior art editor Spencer Holbrook
Jacket coordinator Claire Gell
Jacket designer Natalie Godwin
Jacket design development manager Sophia MTT
Producer, pre-production Jacqueline Street
Producer Vivienne Yong
Managing art editor Philip Letsu
Publisher Andrew Macintyre
Associate publishing director Liz Wheeler
Design director Stuart Jackman
Publishing director Jonathan Metcalf

DK INDIA

Assistant editor Ateendriya Gupta
Art editor Alpana Aditya
DTP designer Pawan Kumar
Senior DTP designer Harish Aggarwal
Picture researcher Sakshi Saluja
Jacket designer Suhita Dharamjit
Managing jackets editor Saloni Singh
Pre-production manager Balwant Singh
Managing editor Kingshuk Ghoshal
Managing art editor Govind Mittal

Two wild
Przewalski's horses

Archer on horseback,
c. fifth century BCE

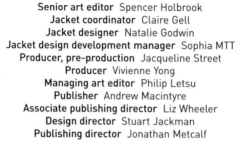

French-style barouche, c.1880

First published in Great Britain in 1992
This revised edition published in Great Britain in 2003, 2008, 2016
by Dorling Kindersley Limited,
80 Strand, London WC2R ORL

Copyright © 1992, 2003, 2008, 2016 Dorling Kindersley Limited
A Penguin Random House Company

10 9 8 7 6 5 4 3 2 1
001 – 294906 – Jun/16

A CIP catalogue record for this book is available
from the British Library

ISBN: 978-0-2412-5885-9

Printed and bound in China

Pair of greys
with English
phaeton, c.1840

A WORLD OF IDEAS:
SEE ALL THERE IS TO KNOW

www.dk.com

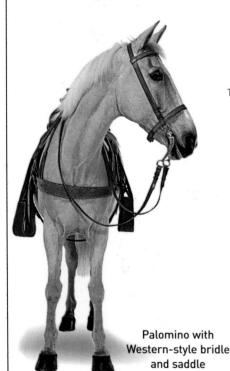

Palomino with
Western-style bridle
and saddle

Contents

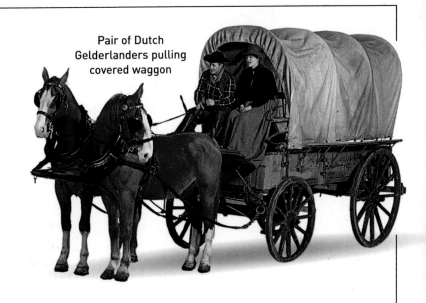

Pair of Dutch
Gelderlanders pulling
covered waggon

The horse family　　　　6

How horses evolved　　　8

Big bones　　　　10

Super senses　　　　12

Mares and foals　　　14

Wild asses　　　　16

Seeing stripes　　　18

Ancient ancestors　　20

Horses in history　　22

Donkey work　　　24

Mules and hinnies　26

New shoes　　　　28

Bits and pieces　　30

Exploring by horse　32

To the Americas　　34

Running wild　　　36

Horses of the world　38

Other breeds and
　　colours　　　　40

War horses　　　　42

The age of chivalry　　44

Travelling by horse　　46

Horse-drawn vehicles　48

Heavy horses　　　50

Horse power　　　52

Light draught work　54

North American equids　56

Sporting horses　　58

Horseplay　　　　60

Useful ponies　　62

Did you know?　　64

Identifying breeds　66

Find out more　　68

Glossary　　　　70

Index　　　　72

The horse family

Horses, asses, and zebras belong to one family of mammals named the "Equidae". They are called "odd-toed" animals because they have only one hoof on each foot, whereas cows and deer have two hooves and are called "even-toed". The Equidae are classified in the order Perissodactyla, alongside rhinoceroses and tapirs. All members of the horse family (equids) feed on grasses and shrubs, live in family groups, and use speed to escape predators. Domestic horses vary in size but they all belong to one species – *Equus caballus*. The various parts of a horse are called the "points" of the horse.

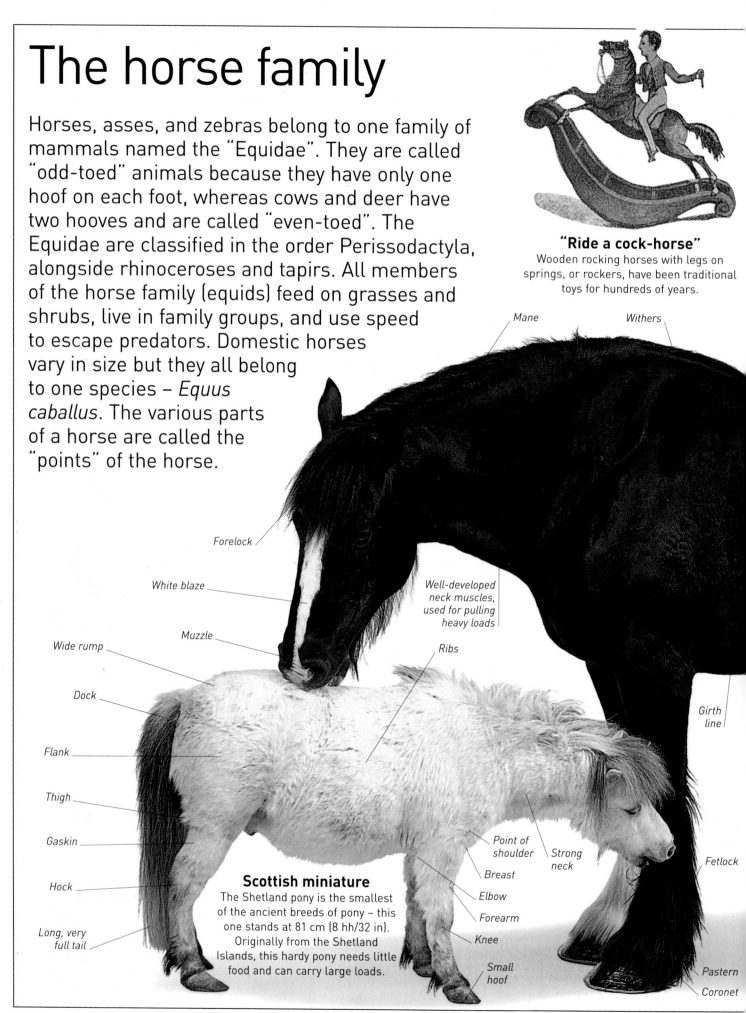

"Ride a cock-horse"
Wooden rocking horses with legs on springs, or rockers, have been traditional toys for hundreds of years.

Mane

Withers

Forelock

White blaze

Muzzle

Well-developed neck muscles, used for pulling heavy loads

Ribs

Wide rump

Dock

Girth line

Flank

Thigh

Gaskin

Point of shoulder

Strong neck

Hock

Breast

Elbow

Forearm

Knee

Fetlock

Long, very full tail

Scottish miniature
The Shetland pony is the smallest of the ancient breeds of pony – this one stands at 81 cm (8 hh/32 in). Originally from the Shetland Islands, this hardy pony needs little food and can carry large loads.

Small hoof

Pastern

Coronet

Large ears with dark tips

No forelock

Heavy head

Dark muzzle

Short, erect mane

Long, erect ears

Typical white muzzle

Pale brown shadow striping between black stripes

Asses and zebras
Other than the horse, the other members of the horse family are the Asian wild asses, the African wild asses, and the zebras.

Pale underbelly

Dark muzzle

Kulan – a type of Asian wild ass

Poitou donkey

Common, or plains, zebra mother and foal

Broad back

Very powerful rump

Measuring a horse's height
The height of a horse is measured in "hands" from the feet to the shoulders ("withers"). One hand (the width of an adult's hand) is equal to 10.16 cm (4 in). A horse measuring 15.2 hh (hands high) is 157 cm (62 in) high.

Short tail prevents snagging in harness

A great horse
The Shire horse was first bred in the English Midlands for work on farms and for pulling great weights. This breed is distinguished by its huge size and by the long hair, or "feathering", around the feet. The horse shown here, called "King", once held the record for the tallest horse in the world – with a height at the withers of 198 cm (19.2 hh/78 in).

A unicorn is a mythical horned horse. In heraldry, this "horse" had a lion's tail, two-toed hooves, and a spiral horn.

Feathered feet

Huge hoof

European travellers
Africa is the ancestral home of many members of the horse family, from zebras to wild asses. Europeans explored this vast continent, bringing domesticated horses to use as transport. This wooden carving was made by Ibo people in Nigeria, West Africa.

How horses evolved

It took about 55 million years for the present family of horses, asses, and zebras (equids) to evolve from their earliest horse-like ancestor. Originally called *Eohippus*, it is now known as *Hyracotherium*. In the woods of Europe, North America, and eastern Asia, this small horse was a "browsing" animal, feeding on leaves and shrubs, with four hoofed toes on its front feet and three on its hind feet. Over millions of years, it became a "grazing" (grass-eating) mammal with three hoofed toes, and later with a single hoof, on all feet. As grassland replaced woodland in North America, ancestral horses evolved longer limbs to escape predators and high-crowned teeth to chew tough grass. The first grazing horse was *Merychippus*, which was replaced by *Pliohippus*, the first one-toed horse, and later gave rise to *Equus*.

Side toe

Hoof of side toe

Main hoof-core

Side view of left hind foot of *Hipparion*

Left side toe

Right side hoof

Hoof of small side toe

Main hoof-core

Front view of hind foot of *Hipparion*

Nasal bone

Incisor tooth

Ear bone

Extinct equid

This skeleton is *Hippidion*, an extinct one-toed equid that evolved in Central America and spread to South America. Its descendant, *Onoluppidium*, survived until 12,000 years ago when human hunters moved across the continent at the end of the Ice Age.

Three-toed grazer

Hipparion (side view of skull, above) was the last three-toed equid. This successful grazer had high-crowned teeth, and its fossil remains have been found in Europe, Asia, and Africa. *Hipparion* was not extinct in Africa until about 125,000 years ago.

Incisor for cutting food

Lost incisor

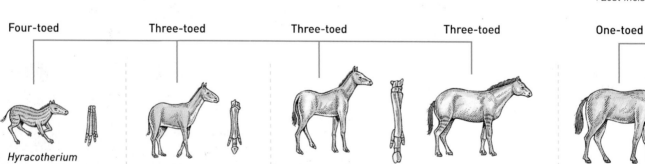

Four-toed	Three-toed	Three-toed	Three-toed	One-toed
Hyracotherium	*Mesohippus*	*Miohippus*	*Merychippus*	*Pliohippus*

Browsers   **Grazers**

Equine sideline

The three-toed fossil horse, *Anchitherium*, spread from America through Asia and Europe about 24 million years ago. However, it was an equine sideline – one that did not evolve into the modern horse. It became extinct five million years ago.

Side toe

Side toe – hoof-core missing

Side hoof-core

Main hoof-core

Lower cheek teeth (molars and premolars)

Foot and toe bones of *Anchitherium*

Lower jaw of *Anchitherium*

Part of mandible (jaw bone)

Upper cheek teeth

Upper jaw of *Anchitherium*

Orbit, or eye socket

Palatal bone

Cranium for brain

The oldest equid

The palatal (roof of mouth) view of this *Hyracotherium* skull from 54 million years ago shows the square, six-lobed teeth from which modern horse teeth evolved.

Palatal view of *Hyracotherium* skull, showing roof of mouth

Parietal bone

Orbit

Nasal bone

Cheek teeth

Side view of right-half of *Hyracotherium* skull

High-crowned teeth used for chewing

Foramen magnum (hole for spinal cord)

Ear bone

Base of cranium

Palatal view of *Hipparion* skull

One-toed

Equus

Grazers

Three-toed first

Sheep-sized *Mesohippus* lived about 37 million years ago and was the first horse to have three toes (with the middle toe larger than the side ones).

9

Cranium (of skull)

Eye socket

Upper molar

Nasal bone

Upper premolar

Incisor, used for cutting food

Lower premolar

Lower jaw, or mandible

Lower molar

Atlas

Axis

Neck vertebra

Incisor teeth are angled forwards, showing old age

Scapula, or shoulder blade

Long in the tooth
As a horse ages, the incisors change from oval to round to triangular and then flattened. The gums also recede, so the horse is "long in the tooth". Experts use these signs to guess a horse's age.

Humerus

Big bones

The skeleton of all members of the horse family is built for speed and stamina. Wild equids use super speed and sharp vision to escape predators. The long skull contains the grinding teeth necessary to chew grass. The vertebral column keeps the back rigid, the rib cage protects the heart and lungs, and the limb bones are extended. Equids run on only a single toe. Foals are often born toothless, but the milk teeth come through the soft jaw bones. These temporary teeth are replaced by adult teeth. An adult equid has 40 teeth – 12 incisors, 4 canines, 12 premolars, and 12 molars. As horses age, their teeth gradually wear down, change shape, and become very discoloured.

Radius

Knee

Metacarpal, or front cannon, bone

First phalanx, or long pastern bone

Second phalanx, or short pastern bone

Hoof

Classic skeleton
In 1766 English artist George Stubbs (1724–1806) published *The Anatomy of the Horse*, which is still used as reference more than 200 years later. He dissected horses to show bone construction.

Skeleton of a racehorse

Upper jaw of new-born horse

Straight from the horse's mouth

Like all mammals, the foal has milk teeth. These wear down as it weans and begins to graze, and are replaced by adult teeth. At first, the adult teeth have short roots and long crowns, but they wear down over time.

Adult molar starting to develop

Milk premolar

Milk canine

Milk incisor

Adult molar starting to develop

Adult molar, ready for cutting

Milk premolar

Adult premolar

Milk incisor

Upper jaw of two-year-old pony

Upper jaw of six-year-old pony

Molar, for grinding food

Premolar, for chewing food

Incisor, for cutting food

Upper jaw of aged horse

Molar almost worn away

Premolar

Incisor

Spinal vertebra

Hip bone

Pelvic girdle

Femur

Tail vertebra

Rib

Stifle joint

Mighty muscles

This anatomical drawing by George Stubbs shows the amazing muscle structure of the horse, which enables it to travel long distances, jump great heights, and haul big loads.

Tibia

Hock joint

Metatarsal, or hind cannon, bone

There are about 25 species of horse chestnut tree in North America, Europe, and Asia. In the late 1500s, the seeds were used to treat respiratory illnesses in horses, so this is how the tree got its name.

Skeleton shape

The shape of a horse's skeleton depends on its breed. A carthorse has huge bones to support the muscles needed to haul heavy weights, while a racehorse (shown above) has long, slender bones built for galloping along at high speed.

First phalanx

Second phalanx

Hoof

Super senses

Rolling over
This pony is having a good roll, as part of grooming. It relaxes the muscles and helps to remove loose hair, dirt, and bugs.

Horses, asses, and zebras have more highly developed senses of sight, hearing, and scent than humans. The long face of the horse is necessary not only for the large teeth, but also the sensitive smell organs. Eyes are set high in the skull on either side of the head, so the horse has all-round vision. Ears are large, and in the asses very long, so they can point towards any sound. The horse is a herd animal showing affection to other group members, and this loyalty is easily transferred to a human owner. This strong bond means horses will follow commands. The domestic horse and donkey retain the natural instincts and behaviour patterns of their wild ancestors, such as defending their territory and suckling their foals.

Ears pointing back show submission or fear

Ears pointing forwards show interest in surroundings

One ear forwards, one ear back shows uncertainty

Two-way stretch
An equid's ears have a dual role – to pick up sounds and transmit visual signals. If a mule (shown above) puts its ears back, it is frightened or angry. If forwards, it is interested in what is happening. One ear forwards and one back means it is not sure what will happen next.

Laid-back ears showing anger

Kick threat

Kulan's kick
The laid-back ears and threatening kicks show that these kulans are not getting along too well.

Zebra calling, responding to the threat from another male

Protecting territory and family
Fighting by rearing and stabbing with the front hooves is natural to all equids. But they can also settle differences by threats with their ears, tails, and feet. Stallions fight over territory or to protect their mares, like these Icelandic ponies.

Cartoon shows lead horse ignoring his driver's commands and taking the liberty of stopping for a drink

Flehmen reaction

Pulling back his lips and drawing air in over his vomero-nasal organ after smelling a mare's urine, this stallion is seeing if she is ready to mate. This is the flehmen reaction.

Bite given to unfamiliar horse

A bite threat

These Przewalski's horses from two different herds are trying to show who is the more dominant, with one showing a bite threat to the other. The attacking horse's neck is thrust forwards ready to bite.

The best of friends

Two horses will often stand close together, head to tail, nuzzling each other's manes and backs, thus establishing their relationship. The frequency of these grooming and cleaning sessions varies from season to season, but they usually last about three minutes.

Ears laid back showing shock of bite attack

Mares and foals

A mare – or mother horse, ass, or zebra – gives birth to one well-developed foal after a carrying-time (gestation period) of about 11 months. The long gestation period ensures the foal is healthy enough to keep up with the herd from birth. Asses, zebras, and horses live on open grasslands where food can be scarce, and the young are an easy target for large predators. The foal stands an hour after birth and begins grazing in weeks. From one to four years, a female foal is called a "filly" and a male foal a "colt". In the wild, fillies and colts leave their mothers' herds to form new groups as they mature.

A pregnant Palomino
The large belly on this Palomino shows she will soon give birth. Pony and feral mares give birth quickly, but highly bred horses are watched in case something goes wrong.

A new-born foal
This mare is resting after giving birth to her foal, which has the birth sac over its back. Soon the foal will kick free from its mother, breaking what was the nourishing umbilical cord.

Licking into shape
The mare has got to her feet and removes the birth sac by licking the foal all over. This also helps strengthen the foal's circulation and breathing.

Foal's erect ears showing alertness

Mother and foal
It will take almost three years for the young foal of this common zebra to become as large as its mother. The family bonds of zebras are very strong and all the adults combine to protect their foals from any danger.

Mother nudging foal away from danger

Six-year-old common zebra mother and three-month-old foal

First drink
As soon as it can stand, the foal finds and sucks the mother's teats. The first milk ("colostrum") helps a foal build immunity to disease.

First steps
While the mother looks around for danger, the foal takes its first faltering steps (right).

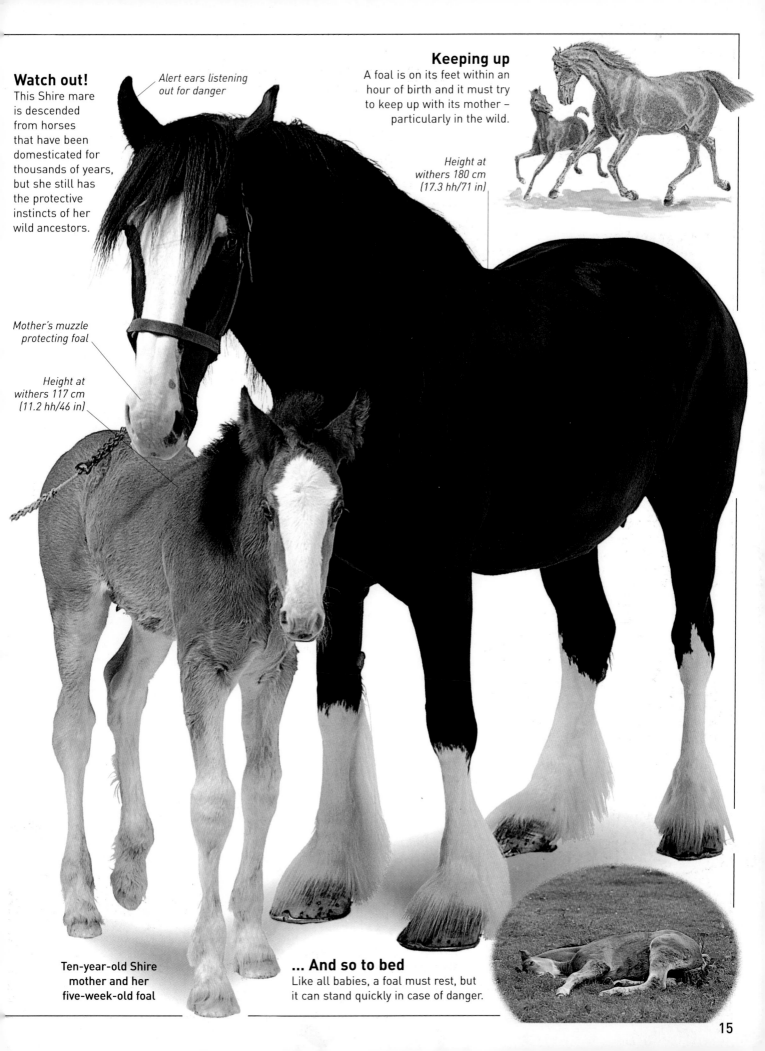

Watch out!
This Shire mare is descended from horses that have been domesticated for thousands of years, but she still has the protective instincts of her wild ancestors.

Alert ears listening out for danger

Mother's muzzle protecting foal

Height at withers 117 cm (11.2 hh/46 in)

Keeping up
A foal is on its feet within an hour of birth and it must try to keep up with its mother – particularly in the wild.

Height at withers 180 cm (17.3 hh/71 in)

Ten-year-old Shire mother and her five-week-old foal

... And so to bed
Like all babies, a foal must rest, but it can stand quickly in case of danger.

Wild asses

There are three species of wild ass, but they are not closely related. They can interbreed, but their offspring will be infertile. The three species are the true wild ass of Africa (*Equus africanus*), which ranged over the Sahara desert in North Africa, and the two species of Asian wild asses – the onager (*Equus hemionus*) from the Middle East and northwest India, and the kiang (*Equus kiang*) from the Tibetan plateau. Of the three, the African wild ass is the ancestor of the domestic donkey. All wild asses look similar, with a heavy head, long ears, short mane, no forelock, slender legs, and a wispy tail. They are adapted for life in the semi-deserts and mountains of Africa and Asia. Today wild asses risk extinction from habitat loss and hunting.

Catch your onager
These scenes of catching wild onagers alive, c. 645 BCE, are from stone friezes in the palace of Nineveh in Assyria. These now-extinct Syrian onagers may have been caught for cross-breeding with domestic donkeys or horses.

Long, wispy tail

Preservation
There were several races of African wild ass until recently. The Somali wild ass (*Equus africanus somaliensis*), the only African ass in the wild, has been taken to an Israeli wildlife park to try to save the species.

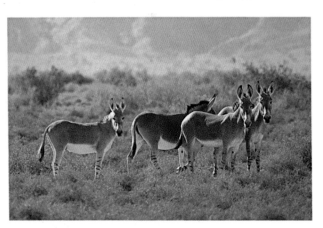

Slender, pale-coloured leg

Now extinct
The Nubian wild ass (*Equus africanus africanus*) is extinct. While the Somali ass has striped legs, the Nubian ass had a dark stripe across its shoulders.

Indian onagers

The Indian onager, or khur (*Equus hemionus khur*), inhabits the Thar Desert. Like all equids, khurs live in groups with an old female as herd leader. Except in mating season, adult males live in separate herds from the females.

Large ears with dark tips

No forelock

Heavy head

Short, erect, mid-brown mane

Dark muzzle

Dark stripe along back

Persian ass

The ghor-khar, or Persian onager (*Equus hemionus onager*), used to live in huge herds that migrated across the deserts in Iran, but today only a very few animals survive in the wild. The onager can gallop at a speed of 48 kph (30 mph) for a long time and can jump over rocks nearly 2 m (7 ft) high.

The kulan

These onagers belong to a subspecies called the kulan (*Equus hemionus kulan*). They live in in the deserts of Turkmenistan. Kulans are 112–122 cm (11–12 hh/44–48 in) in height. In winter they grow a thick coat to protect against the icy winds. Neither the onager nor the kiang has been domesticated, though in the ancient civilizations of the Near East, onagers were probably crossed with donkeys and horses to produce strong hybrids.

Pale, almost white underbelly

Brink of extinction

The kiang (*Equus kiang*), or Tibetan wild ass, is the largest ass, at more than 142 cm (14 hh/56 in) tall. Kiangs are sacred to the Tibetans, but risk extinction from hunting and habitat loss.

Queen Puabi's rein ring features an onager in Ur's royal tombs, in ancient Mesopotamia, c. 2500 BCE.

Seeing stripes

Today, zebras live only in Africa but their ancestors, like all horse family members, evolved in North America. There are three living species of zebra – Grevy's, common, and mountain – in different habitats with different stripe patterns. Zebras feed on coarse grass and cross wide areas to graze. They are very social, spending time on grooming and nuzzling each other. Zebras live in family groups of 100 or more. It is not known why zebras are striped, but the pattern may make it harder for predators to single out one animal when the herd gathers together.

Large, rounded ears

Big ears
The Grevy's large, round ears can signal to other zebras and listen out for distant sounds.

White ears with black tips

Oval ears

Very dark muzzle

Small, squarish dewlap on throat

Thinner stripes down legs

No stripes on belly

Seven-year-old female mountain zebra

Stripes of backbone go down tail

Broad, well-marked stripes over rump

Shadows between stripes

Donkey-like tail, with hair only at its tip

Mountain zebra
The mountain zebra, *Equus zebra* (above), is today an endangered species that may soon be extinct. It is found in small numbers in the mountain ranges of the western Cape province of South Africa and up the west coast to Angola. Like the common zebra, the mountain zebra averages about 132 cm (13 hh/52 in) at the withers.

Six-year-old common, or plains, zebra mare and her three-month-old foal

Zebroid
Zebras can interbreed with all other horse species, but their offspring are infertile. This Zorse is a hybrid between a zebra and a horse.

Common or plains
The common zebra, *Equus burchelli*, at 132 cm (13 hh/52 in), once ranged throughout eastern and southern Africa. Today, it is still widespread and herds can be seen in most wildlife reserves. Young males live in bachelor groups until they form new families.

Dorsal, or back stripe, is broad and black

Very narrow stripes on face

Grevy's zebra

Grevy's zebra, *Equus grevyi*, is the northernmost species inhabiting the semi-desert areas of Kenya, Ethiopia, and Somalia. It is the largest zebra, standing about 142–152 cm (14–15 hh/56–60 in), and is considered to be a relic of more primitive horse family members.

Very tall, erect mane

Rounded ears

No forelock on head

White on either side of black dorsal stripe

V-shaped, brown patch on nose

Two female Grevy's zebras, aged three to four years

Narrow, closely-spaced black stripes on a white background, especially over the withers

White underbelly

Broad hooves

Stripes go down legs, ending in black coronet, next to hoof

Pale brown shadow striping between black stripes

Black dorsal stripe becomes thinner down the tail, with stripes on either side

Stripes bend round, becoming horizontal over haunches

White inside of leg with no stripes

The quagga

A fourth species of zebra, the quagga (*Equus quagga*), was found by 19th-century explorers in southern Africa. Quaggas were hunted to extinction, but attempts are now being made to recreate the species by selectively breeding plains zebras.

Zedonk

Cross-breeding between a zebra and a donkey can produce finely-striped brown animals, such as these zedonks from Zimbabwe. Many zoos have successful cross-breeding programmes.

Ancient ancestors

Fossil evidence reveals that at the end of the last Ice Age, 10,000 years ago, millions of horses lived wild across Europe and Asia. They belonged to one species, *Equus ferus*, that roamed in herds and made annual migrations. As grassland replaced forest, horse numbers dropped from habitat loss and hunting until few wild horses were left. The first wild horses were tamed and domesticated in Asia and eastern Europe about 6,000 years ago, soon spreading westward. All the domestic horses in the world today are descended from these domesticated ancestors and they are classified in one species, called *Equus caballus*.

Extinct wild horse
Many 18th-century travellers to Russia saw small wild horses, called tarpan (*Equus ferus ferus*). They died out in the early 1800s. In Poland today, ponies similar to the tarpan have been bred from primitive breeds, such as the konik.

Height range at withers of 132–142 cm (13–14 hh/ 52–56 in)

Short mane

Short forelock

An ancient English pony
The Exmoor pony is an ancient breed that closely resembles the extinct tarpan, or wild pony, of eastern Europe. The ponies live in feral herds on Exmoor in England.

Light-coloured muzzle, typical of wild horse

Sacred white horse
White horses were sacred to the Celts of western Europe. In about 500 BCE a horse shape was scraped into the chalk hills at Uffington in England.

Lumbar vertebra

Hip bone

Scapula

Atlas, or first vertebra

Cranium

Eye socket

Nasal bone

Axis

Lower jaw

Neck vertebra

Upper cheek teeth

Femur

Tail vertebra

Stifle joint

Rib

Humerus

Radius

Hock joint

Metatarsal bone

Metacarpal bone

Knee

Skeleton of a Przewalski's horse
Przewalski's horse is built for speed. The long and slender bones are attached to each other by ligaments, which are strong and elastic so the joints move easily. The framework of the skeleton is covered with powerful muscles and little fat.

Przewalski's horses
Wild Przewalski's horses (*Equus ferus przewalskii*) were found in Mongolia in the 1880s, with a few bred in European zoos. They have been extinct in the wild since the 1960s, but are being reintroduced to Mongolia from herds bred in captivity.

Cave paintings
This wild horse (*Equus ferus*) was painted on a wall in the famous caves at Lascaux in France by hunting people towards the end of the last Ice Age, about 14,000 years ago.

Long, shaggy tail

Group of Przewalski's horses

Wild African ass
The African wild ass (*Equus africanus*) is the ancestor of all domestic donkeys. It is still found in very small numbers in the eastern Sahara, but it is in danger of extinction.

Horses in history

The earliest evidence for the domestication of the horse comes from the Ukraine, where people lived by herding horses and cattle on the grass steppes 6,000 years ago. At this time, the African wild ass was being domesticated in ancient Egypt and Arabia. Horses and asses were harnessed in a pair to a chariot. These chariots became a status symbol of kings, who used them for battles, parades, and hunting. By the 8th century BCE, riding horses and donkeys was a popular means of travel. The ancient Greeks and Romans built special sporting arenas for chariot races.

The end of the day
This horse's head is from the Parthenon marbles (5th century BCE) in Athens, Greece. Legend goes that horses pulled the Sun's chariot to the sea each day to make the sunset, so the horse's face looks exhausted.

Royal standard
This early depiction of donkeys harnessed to a cart is on a mosaic box – the Standard of Ur – in the royal tombs of Ur in ancient Mesopotamia.

Flying through the air
In Greek mythology, Pegasus was a winged horse, springing from the blood of Medusa when Perseus, a son of Zeus, cut off her head. The horse flew to join the gods, but was caught by Athena, goddess of wisdom, and tamed with a golden bridle. This engraving of Pegasus on a bronze container was made by the Etruscans in about 300 BCE.

Half man, half horse
The myth of the centaurs – half men and half horses – may come from sightings of the horsemen of Thessaly in ancient Greece. People were unfamiliar with men on horseback, so they thought this was a new being. This scene shows the battles between the wild centaurs and the Lapiths of northern Greece.

Ready for war
This terracotta model from Cyprus shows an Assyrian warrior. His horse has a breastplate and headdress.

The four horses of Venice

Thought to be the work of 4th-century-BCE Greek sculptor, Lysippus, these bronze horses were taken from Constantinople (now Istanbul) in 1204 CE, to the San Marco Basilica in Venice.

Brand mark

Brands on horses have been used as proof of ownership for more than 2,000 years. This hunting scene is from a mosaic pavement (c. late 5th or 6th century BCE) discovered at Carthage, a city founded by the Phoenicians near modern-day Tunis. The mosaic was made in North Africa and shows a favourite pastime of wealthy landowners – hunting.

Surprise!

During the Trojan War of 1184 BCE, the Greeks invaded Troy by hiding soldiers inside an enormous wooden horse. The Trojans later famously wheeled the horse into the city.

A bit of a Tang

The people of China have always had a great respect for their horses. During the Tang Dynasty (618–907 CE), many earthenware models of horses were produced that are of great artistic value today. The cobalt-blue glaze was very rare and expensive to produce at that time, because cobalt was imported only in very small quantities. This figure would have been moulded in several parts and then joined together as a whole.

Donkey work

The domesticated ass, or donkey (*Equus asinus*), is descended from the African wild ass (*Equus africanus*), which inhabits the hot deserts of the Sahara and Arabia. In such a harsh environment, the donkey has developed strength, stamina, and endurance to help it carry heavy loads long distances on little food and water. In the wild, donkey foals develop quickly to keep up with the herd when it travels in search of bushes and grass. Female donkeys, or jennies, carry their foals for 12 months before birth. Like all horse family members, the donkey thrives in groups.

Jesus on a donkey
When baby Jesus was born, donkey was the usual means of transport in Jerusalem. The "cross" on a donkey's back – a stripe along the backbone and band across the shoulders – combined with the fact that Jesus rode a donkey on the first Palm Sunday, made people believe that these hairs had healing powers.

Donkey herders
In Andalusia, Spain, donkeys are still used to help with herding and farm work.

Greek harvest
In Greece, until recently, it was a common sight to see donkeys threshing grain. By walking round in a circle, the donkeys' hooves separate the seeds and husks.

Water, water
Water is the most precious resource in desert countries. This Tunisian woman is leading her donkey, loaded with water jars.

Rein

Breeching straps (that go around animal's haunches)

Wooden shaft

Footstand for stepping up into cart

Mid-19th-century English donkey cart

Long ears help keep donkey cool

Typical white muzzle

Lighter baby or juvenile coat on back

Darker adult coat, like his father's, now visible at first moulting

Poitou donkeys

For centuries in the Poitou region of France and in Spain, there has been a tradition of breeding large donkeys to mate with female horses and produce giant mules for farm work. Poitou donkeys stand 142 cm (14 hh/56 in) at the shoulder, or withers, making them the world's largest donkeys. They have long, shaggy coats.

White underbelly

Long, slender legs

A family group: five-year-old father, nine-year-old mother, and 11-month-old son

This poor old donkey has had a hard-working life and now deserves a peaceful retirement.

Ten-year-old Irish donkey, at 117 cm (11.2 hh/46 in)

Terret

Rein ring

Bridle

Decorated brow band

Blinker

Nose band

Bit

Collar

Trace

Girth strap

African donkeys

These donkeys are drinking from a waterhole in Kenya where they live semi-wild on a ranch. They must fend for themselves and learn to keep away from predators.

Long ears

Long tail, with tuft at tip

Well-trimmed hooves

Donkeys of Ireland

Donkeys are the traditional pack and haulage animals of Ireland – one of the few countries in northern Europe where they have been bred for centuries, and where they have adapted to a climate very different from the deserts in which they evolved. Irish donkeys have thicker coats and much shorter legs than donkeys from hotter regions.

Regal white donkeys

Donkeys are popular pets on farm parks. This has led to breeding for new looks, like these white donkeys. In ancient times, white donkeys were favoured by royalty.

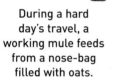

Breast collar (easier to fit than larger collar, as chest is so narrow)

Long, ass-like ears of its father

During a hard day's travel, a working mule feeds from a nose-bag filled with oats.

Mules and hinnies

The Sumerians of Mesopotamia were the first people to interbreed horses and donkeys to produce mules (donkey father, horse mother) and hinnies (horse father, donkey mother) about 4,000 years ago. For thousands of years mules have been used as pack animals to carry huge loads, because they combine donkey stamina with horse strength. Like its parents, a mule is a herd animal that travels best in a "mule train" (a long line of mules harnessed together to pull loads). All the species in the horse family can interbreed, but the resulting offspring will be sterile.

Ancient Egyptian equids
This ancient Egyptian tomb painting from c. 1400 BCE shows a pair of horses drawing a chariot, while below two white hinnies are also pulling one. Their smaller ears show they are hinnies, not mules.

Crate of ducks

Large wheel makes it easier for donkey to pull this load

Indian travel
Mule carts have been used in Asia for 3,000 years. Early carts were attached by a wooden pole to a pair of mules, or horses. The idea of putting an animal between two wooden shafts was only invented 2,000 years ago. Above, the mule has a bridle with a bit and is driven with reins. The family's goods are piled into the cart.

14-year-old mule, 140 cm (13.3 hh/55 in), drawing Indian cart (c. 1840)

A powerful mule

Mules travelled faster than oxen and were more sure-footed than horses, so 19th-century settlers preferred these animals for hauling huge loads over very muddy roads on their long trek west across North America.

Large body

Heavy head with long ears

Neat front legs

Strong hind legs

Long tail, like a horse

No forelock, like a donkey

Short ears

Typical short donkey-like mane

Tourist class

People will always enjoy a leisurely drive in a carriage and even in the busy streets of today's large cities this is still possible. This mule, hitched to a post decorated with a horse's head, is waiting patiently to take tourists around New Orleans, USA.

Cross-breeding

When a donkey is crossed with a horse, the foal has what is called "hybrid vigour" – meaning it is stronger and healthier than either of its parents. The most common cross-breed is a donkey stallion (or jack-ass) with a horse mare, which produces a "mule", but if a horse stallion is crossed with a female donkey (or jenny) the hybrid offspring is called a "hinny" (or jennet). Generally, a mule is a stronger animal than a hinny.

Stubborn as a hinny

This eight-year-old white hinny (whose parents were a female donkey and a pony stallion) will not be pulled where it does not want to go. Donkeys, mules, and hinnies have a reputation for being stubborn, but this is because their behavioural patterns are not understood correctly. These intelligent herd animals are nervous of going to new places alone. Once they are trained to follow a person, they will go anywhere.

Dark grey spots on white, short-haired coat

Long, tufted tail, used for swishing flies, or to show it is anxious

Misbehaving mule

Eight-year-old hinny

New shoes

1 Remove old shoe
The horse stands patiently while the farrier carefully levers off the worn old shoe.

Equid hooves are made of "keratin", a protein like hair or human finger nails. Hooves can be cut and shaped without hurting the animal. On flat land, horse hooves wear down evenly, but on stony ground, hooves split and break, while on soft ground, hooves grow long and diseased. A horse receives regular attention from a "farrier", a person trained to look after hooves and fit protective metal shoes. The hoof consists of the outer "wall", the "sole", and wedge-shaped "frog".

Old horseshoe and nails just removed from horse's hoof by farrier

Indian shoes
Methods of shoeing horses have been the same worldwide for centuries. In this drawing, three workers are shoeing a horse during the time of the Mughal emperors in northern India, c. 1600 CE.

Girth's powerful muscles enable horse to do very heavy work

Feathering on foot

Shoeing a four-year-old Shire horse

Farrier's box of essential tools for shoeing horses

Good luck

A horseshoe is a lucky talisman. It is held with the open part at the top, so good luck does not drop out. Horseshoe pitching – a game of luck – is played in the USA and Canada.

"Horn", or horseshoe-shaped excess hoof growth, removed by farrier

2 Hoof clean

The excess hoof is clipped and the hoof is filed and cleaned so it is ready for the new shoe.

3 At the forge

The farrier makes a new iron shoe at the forge. Using a heavy hammer, the farrier shapes the shoe on an anvil and adds holes for the nails.

4 Steaming

At the stables, the shoe is reheated, pressed onto the hoof to check the fit, and then allowed to cool down. The hoof gives off a smell of burning hair and much smoke, but this does not hurt the horse.

Height at withers 178 cm (17.2 hh/ 70 in)

Chestnut

6 Finished foot

The foot rim is filed before the farrier hammers it flat. Nails must be flush with the shoe, and the hoof and the outer shoe edge should match.

Balancing on one front foot

Filing hoof and nail ends flat

5 Nailing on the shoe

The farrier hammers special iron nails through pre-drilled holes in the shoe. Nail ends showing through the hoof are wrung off and turned back.

When "hippo" meant "horse"

Before iron horseshoes, the Romans tied a shoe of wicker or metal to the hoof with leather, called a "hipposandal" (*hippo* in Greek means "horse").

Hipposandal, French, 1st–3rd century CE

Bits and pieces

The earliest domestic horses and asses were ridden bareback and guided by a rope tied around the lower jaw. This is still the way to control donkeys in Turkey and Greece. The first bits, or bridles' mouthpieces with fastenings at each end to which reins are attached, were made of hide, bone, or wood. In about 1500 BCE, bronze and then iron replaced them. Until late Roman times, horsemen rode bareback. There were no saddles or stirrups (loops suspended from a saddle to support the rider's foot) in Europe until the 8th century CE. This didn't stop Eurasian or native American horsemen shooting arrows from a galloping horse. The most powerful ancient nomadic horsemen were the Scythians of Central Asia in the 4th century BCE.

Back view of woman riding side-saddle

Jingle bells
Bells on the harness were a safety feature. If riders got lost, the chimes could be heard by rescuers.

Spurred on
Horses in 13th-century Europe had a hard time, for they were bridled with bits and goaded by armoured knights wearing cruel spurs (U-shaped devices attached to the rider's boot heel).

Rowel spur (length 23 cm/9 in), made of iron and brass, western European, early 1500s

Rowel

Screw would have clamped stirrup to outside of shoe

Metal part of stirrup would have fitted inside heel of shoe

Tiny rowel spur (length 4 cm/1.5 in), made of iron and fitting directly onto shoe, European, late 1600s

Buckle for attaching stirrup to boot

Metal part of stirrup for "pricking" horse

Prick spur (total length 29 cm/11 in), made of iron, Moorish, early 1800s

Putting your foot in it
The Chinese probably invented metal foot stirrups in the 5th century CE. Stirrups spread westwards to Europe. They influenced the battlefield, allowing horsemen to wield their weapons without falling off.

Iron stirrup, Bulgar, 800–900 CE

Decorated boot stirrup, made of iron, Spanish, 1600s

Brass fretwork

Box stirrup, made of painted wood and brass fretwork, French or Italian, late 1700s

Dragon decoration

Brass stirrup, decorated with two dragons, Chinese, 1800s

Build a better bit

Three types of bit control domesticated horses. The first is the simple "snaffle" bit, developed into a jointed mouthpiece in Assyria, c. 900 BCE. A "curb" bit is unjointed with a chain under the horse's chin, which applies pressure with reins. A "pelham" bit combines two bits of a double bridle in one.

Joint *Rein ring*

Jointed snaffle bit, Irish, 100 BCE–100 CE

Detail from the Bayeux tapestry from France, c. 1080

Defeat in battle

In the Battle of Hastings, 1066 CE, William the Conqueror's troops beat the English. One reason for victory was their use of stirrups, while the English dismounted to fight on foot.

Joint *Rein ring*

Jointed snaffle bit with cheekpiece, Bulgar, 800–900 CE

Cheekpiece

Curb chain *Double rollers in horse's mouth* *Rein ring*

Brass boss

Curb bit made of steel and brass, European, 1500s

Brass boss

Curb chain *Rein ring* *Mouthpiece*

Curb bit made of steel and brass, Portuguese, 1800s

Brow band *Headpiece* *Throatlatch*

Height at withers 173 cm (17 hh/ 68 in)

Rein

Bit

Side-saddle

This grey Lipizzaner gelding is being ridden side-saddle. Women today usually only ride like this in the show ring or out hunting. In former times, from the early 1300s onwards, the side-saddle was the only way a female rider, wearing long, heavy skirts, could be mounted on a horse.

Girth *Safety stirrup* *Rider on leather saddle made-to-measure in 1890*

Woman, in Victorian dress, riding side-saddle on a six-year-old Lipizzaner

Rein ring (terret), English, 1st century CE

Strap-union made of bronze (for joining straps together), English, 1st century CE

Decorated terret (a ring on saddle harness through which driving reins pass), found in Egypt, 1st century BCE

Exploring by horse

Viking chessman
This 12th-century knight on horseback carving is one of the famous chessmen from Scotland's Isle of Lewis.

Without the horse and the ass, human history would have been quite different. Civilizations would have evolved in their places of origin and people could not have explored and conquered. An invading force must have fast transport and efficient movement of goods, weapons, and food, otherwise it is powerless against the defences of settled communities. Although horseriding was the common form of transport from 1000 BCE, it wasn't until the 11th century CE that horses were shod, and a saddle and stirrups used. From this time, the horse became important in war, sport, and travel.

Genghis Khan
Genghis Khan (1162–1227 CE), the Mongolian conqueror, ruled an empire of nomadic horsemen that stretched across Asia into Europe.

Statue of Charlemagne, the Holy Roman Emperor

Pair of bronze Etruscan riders, c. 500 BCE

Archers of the ancient world
These two Etruscan bronzes from Italy show how Scythian archers shot arrows from galloping horses. The archer shooting backwards exemplifies the "Parthian shot", a technique used by nomadic horsemen on the steppes of central Asia.

Holy Roman Emperor
Charlemagne, or Charles the Great (742–814 CE), was the most famous ruler of the Middle Ages. In 796 CE, he led 15,000 horsemen against the Avars in Hungary, and later became Emperor of the Holy Roman Empire.

Fretwork

In the saddle
This 18th-century wooden saddle is probably similar to the one used by Genghis Khan 600 years before.

Tree

Cantle

Pommel

18th-century Tibetan saddle

Alexander the Great

Bucephalus, a black stallion born c. 331 BCE, is probably the most famous horse to have ever lived. He belonged to Alexander the Great (356–323 BCE), and together they conquered much of the known world – from Greece to Egypt and Afghanistan.

Stone frieze of Alexander the Great on his horse, Bucephalus (left), on a sarcophagus in Syria

Patron saint

St George is England and Portugal's patron saint.

Archer showing "Parthian shot"

Tassel on bridle

Curb ring

Curb chain

Gold embroidery on felt, stitched onto leather backing

Reins

Golden wonder

This exquisite gold model of a four-horse chariot, c. 5th century BCE, is from the Achaemenid Empire of Persia (now Iran).

Part of treasure found near the River Oxus in central Asia

Early 19th-century North African bridle with curb bit

To the Americas

Before 1492, when European settlers arrived in North and South America, the continents were inhabited by native people, who had arrived about 15,000 years earlier. European invaders had fast horses and mules, and they conquered the land. A few horses escaped to live and breed in the wild, and a century later, they had spread over the grasslands. Native Americans soon saw the value of the horse. They bartered with the Spanish for their own stock and learned to ride like the ancient horsemen.

Fine hats
America's Sioux chieftains ride their most beautiful horses for ceremonial occasions.

The Black Hawk war
The Sauk Indians prized their horses for transport, hunting, and war. US officials made Keokuk (above, c. 1760–1848) Sauk chief and he signed treaties giving away Sauk land. Black Hawk, the Sauks' true leader, defended the land, but was defeated. Millions of acres of Indian territory were ceded to the whites.

Beasts of burden
Before there were railways across North America, teams of mules would haul heavy wagons along muddy roads that were impassable by any other means of transport.

Blaze

Central wooden shaft, or "tongue", to which harness is attached

Down Mexico way
In the early 1500s, Spanish conquistadors took horses to the New World, where they had been extinct for 10,000 years. Here Indians give Mexican conqueror Hernando Cortés (1485–1547) a necklace.

Martingale

Stocking

Shod hoof gives better grip

Westward ho!

Trappers, traders, and missionaries were the first to reach the Pacific, but in 1843 a determined band of 1,000 settlers left Missouri on the 3,300-km (2,000-mile) trek westwards along the Oregon Trail. Finally, after many gruelling months, they reached their destination.

Canvas held up by iron hoop underneath

Waterproof heavy-duty canvas top

Brake lever

Axle supporting the weight of wagon and load

Iron rim over wooden wheel

Whippletree, attaching harness to wagon

Metal hub

Trace

Pair of Gelderlanders (168 cm/16.2 hh/66 in)

Mobile home

Early European settlers travelled across North America in a covered wagon, or "prairie schooner". They had to be entirely self-sufficient, knowing how to shoe a horse, mend a wheel, and bake bread.

Front wheel, 123 cm (4 ft) across, is smaller for sharp turns

Cowboys

The horsemen, or gauchos, of the South American pampas work on huge ranches. They spend their lives in the saddle.

Running wild

There are no longer any truly wild horses, but all over the world there are many herds of horses and ponies described as "feral". These feral animals are descended from domesticated stock, but they live and breed in the wild. The last truly wild horses were the Przewalski's horses that survived in Mongolia until the 1960s. In North and South America, horses spread rapidly over the grasslands after the first Europeans brought horses and donkeys in the 15th century. Soon large herds of horses and donkeys were living wild all over the grassland and deserts.

Fell ponies
In Britain many breeds of pony live on the moors, like the Fell pony. Although Fell ponies are owned, they can live and breed with little human control.

Long ears

Well-proportioned head

Coat colours vary from bay, brown, and grey, but never piebald or skewbald

German Dülmen
These rare ponies live semi-wild on the Duke of Croy's estate in Westphalia in Germany. They have been cross-bred with British and Polish ponies, so they are not pure-bred. The herd dates back to the 1300s.

Strong legs support sturdy, well-built body

Well-formed feet with strong horn

The brumby of Australia
There have been feral horses in Australia for 150 years, ever since they were abandoned during the gold rush. Called brumbies, these horses reproduced in big numbers over vast areas. Since the 1960s, they have been hunted to such an extent that there are now very few.

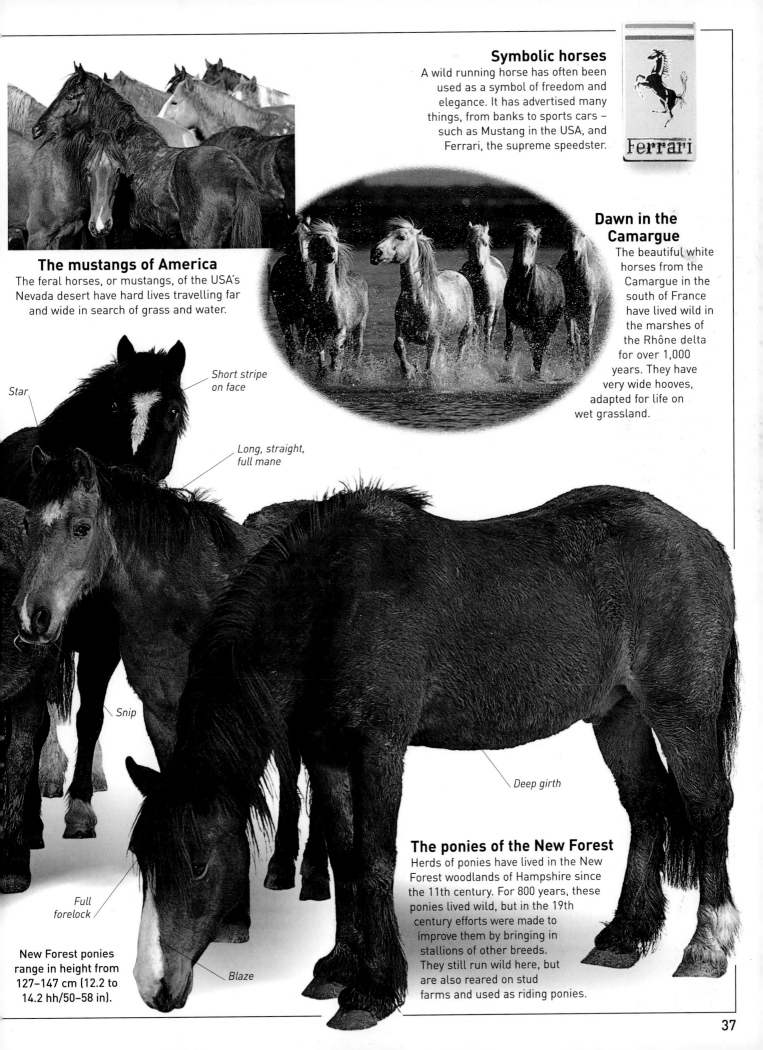

Symbolic horses

A wild running horse has often been used as a symbol of freedom and elegance. It has advertised many things, from banks to sports cars – such as Mustang in the USA, and Ferrari, the supreme speedster.

The mustangs of America

The feral horses, or mustangs, of the USA's Nevada desert have hard lives travelling far and wide in search of grass and water.

Dawn in the Camargue

The beautiful white horses from the Camargue in the south of France have lived wild in the marshes of the Rhône delta for over 1,000 years. They have very wide hooves, adapted for life on wet grassland.

Star

Short stripe on face

Long, straight, full mane

Snip

Deep girth

The ponies of the New Forest

Herds of ponies have lived in the New Forest woodlands of Hampshire since the 11th century. For 800 years, these ponies lived wild, but in the 19th century efforts were made to improve them by bringing in stallions of other breeds. They still run wild here, but are also reared on stud farms and used as riding ponies.

Full forelock

New Forest ponies range in height from 127–147 cm (12.2 to 14.2 hh/50–58 in).

Blaze

Horses of the world

Breeds of horse are often divided by breeders into three types. First are "hotbloods" – the Arab and Thoroughbred breeds. This name is a result of their descent from the Arab and Barb breeds of hot countries in North Africa and Arabia. Second are "coldbloods", which are the heavy draught horses of cold, northern climates. Third are "warmbloods", which are crosses between hotbloods and coldbloods. This group supplies most modern sports horses, except racehorses, which are Thoroughbreds. All Thoroughbreds can trace their ancestry to three stallions: Byerly Turk (c. 1689), Darley Arabian (c. 1702), and Godolphin Arabian (c. 1731).

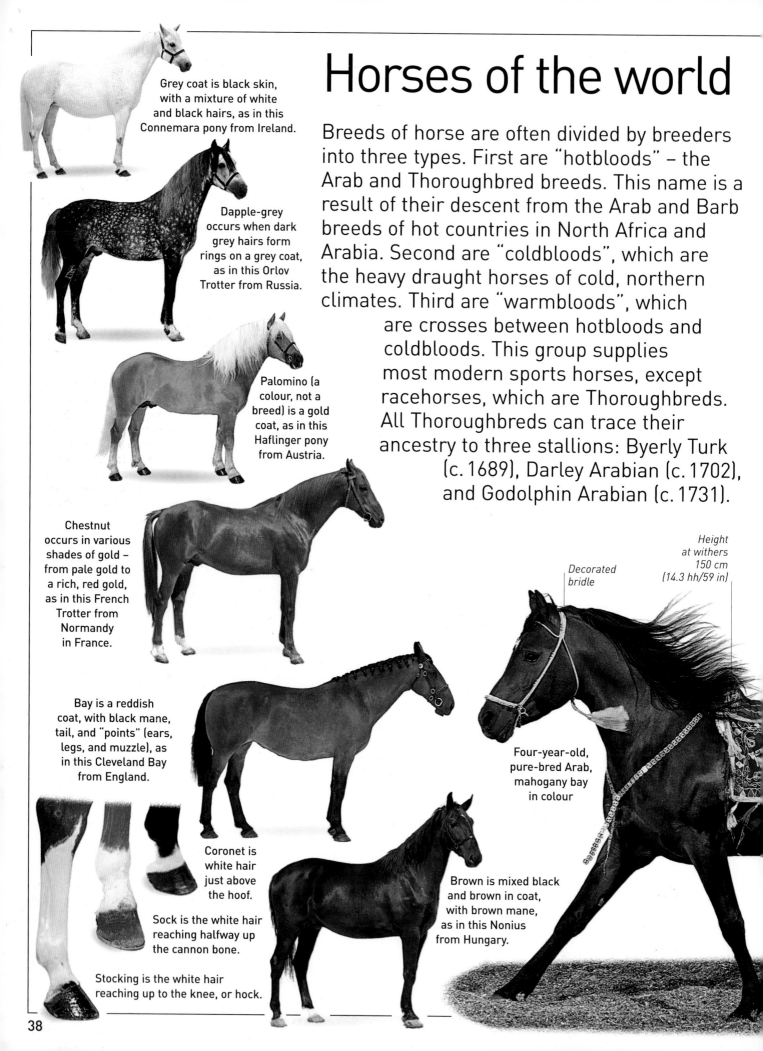

Grey coat is black skin, with a mixture of white and black hairs, as in this Connemara pony from Ireland.

Dapple-grey occurs when dark grey hairs form rings on a grey coat, as in this Orlov Trotter from Russia.

Palomino (a colour, not a breed) is a gold coat, as in this Haflinger pony from Austria.

Chestnut occurs in various shades of gold – from pale gold to a rich, red gold, as in this French Trotter from Normandy in France.

Bay is a reddish coat, with black mane, tail, and "points" (ears, legs, and muzzle), as in this Cleveland Bay from England.

Coronet is white hair just above the hoof.

Sock is the white hair reaching halfway up the cannon bone.

Stocking is the white hair reaching up to the knee, or hock.

Brown is mixed black and brown in coat, with brown mane, as in this Nonius from Hungary.

Decorated bridle

Height at withers 150 cm (14.3 hh/59 in)

Four-year-old, pure-bred Arab, mahogany bay in colour

38

Barbs and Berbers
The Barb, second only to the Arab as the first horse breed, is the traditional mount of North African tribesmen, called Berbers.

Moroccan horsemen ride at a festival

Rearing up
As horses are beautiful and can be trained easily, they are used in circus shows, where they can show unusual movements with their bodies.

Height at withers 145 cm (14.1 hh/57 in)

Coats of many colours
In this painting by Indian artists from the Mughal school (c. 1590), a crow addresses an assembly of animals in a Persian fable. The horses' coat colours are chestnut, light and dappled greys, bay, and skewbald.

15-year-old Arab, very light grey colour with tiny dapples in coat

Horse fair
Horses have been sold at horse sales for centuries, as shown in this detail of a painting by English artist, John Herring (1795–1865).

Aristocratic Arab
The Arab is the aristocrat of horses, with an elegant head, slender limbs, and fiery nature. Arabs have been carefully bred, and records kept of their pedigrees in both North Africa and Arabia.

Embroidered saddle-cloth

Other breeds and colours

Every country has its own breed of horse, adapted to life in its place of origin. Breeds are defined by their "conformation", or size and body shape, as well as colour and any white markings on the face and legs. Horses come in different sizes – from the smallest horse, the Falabella, which measures 76 cm (7.2 hh/30 in) at the withers, to the largest breed, the Shire horse. A Shire stallion stands 168 cm (16.2 hh/66 in) and weighs about a tonne. Many sayings link horse behaviour to coat colours. There is an Arab saying that all horses but bays are unlucky, unless they have white markings, and another that a white horse is the most princely, but suffers in heat.

Height at withers 165 cm (16.1 hh/65 in)

Flat metal stirrup

Stars...
It is usual for horses to have white facial markings, such as a regular, or irregular, "star" shape high on the face. An example is this Danish Warmblood, a breed now regarded as Denmark's national horse.

... And stripes
A strip of white, extending from above the eyes to the nostrils, is called a "stripe", as on this Oldenburg, a breed established in Germany in the 1600s.

What the blazes!
A wide strip above the eyes and extending down the muzzle is a "blaze", as on this Gelderlander from the Netherlands. When white hair covers almost all the face, it is called a "white face".

Seven-year-old, dark grey, pure-bred Andalusian ridden by a woman in classical Spanish riding costume

Classical equitation
The Spanish Riding School was founded in 1572 with Lipizzaner horses.

Horses in art

The beauty and strength of the horse has inspired sculptors and artists for thousands of years, such as this stylized work by German painter, Franz Marc (1880–1916).

The "Spanish Horse"

Known as the "Spanish Horse" for centuries, Andalusian horses were first bred by Carthusian monks at Spanish monasteries in the 1400s. Today's horses are bay or grey, but they were originally chestnut or black.

Numnah (sheepskin pad to protect horse's back)

Spanish-style saddle blanket

Exhibiting spectacular passage, a slow-tempo trot with exaggerated elevation of legs

Horses are called black when the coat, mane, tail, and legs are completely black, as in this Friesian from the Netherlands.

Roan colour can be "strawberry" (where the coat colour is chestnut with white hairs mixed), or "blue" (a black or brown coat with some white hair), as in this Italian Heavy Draught horse from Italy.

Dun colour can be a blue, mouse, or light yellow coat (with black in the legs, mane, and tail), as in this Norwegian Fjord pony. The "dorsal eel stripe" seen on the mane and back is typical of this breed.

A spotted coat can have five varieties of pattern, usually dark spots on light hair, as seen here in this minute Falabella, first bred in Argentina.

Skewbald means white patches on another coat colour. This Pinto pony has a chestnut coat with white patches ("Ovaro"), but a white coat with coloured patches is called "Tobiano".

Piebald means large, irregular patches of white and black hairs in the coat, as in this Shetland pony.

War horses

The horse and the ass have been used by people to assist in wars for 5,000 years. By riding in chariots harnessed to a pair of horses, men could travel fast and cause damage to the enemy. Minor squabbles between individuals became battles as families expanded and villages were settled. When armed horseriders (cavalry) arrived at the time of Alexander the Great, the horse played a big role in all wars until after World War I, when mechanized vehicles took over. As higher, steady saddles were introduced, longer weapons could easily be used on the battlefield.

Napoleon's favourite
Marengo was the white Arab pony ridden by French leader, Napoleon Bonaparte (1769–1821) at the Battle of Waterloo in Belgium in 1815, when he was defeated by the British.

Rider's uniform embroidered with real gold thread

Royal coat of arms (featuring a lion and a unicorn) embroidered with gold and silver threads on damask silk of drum banner

Made of pure silver, these drums weigh 68 kg (150 lb)

Bridle's beard, or tussle, made of natural horse hair – black hair surrounding dyed red hair

Double reins covered with real gold thread – boot reins connected to rider's stirrups, second set to rider's waist

Tilting at windmills
In 1605, Spanish poet Miguel de Cervantes (1547–1616) created his memorable character, Don Quixote, and his mare, Rocinante. He and his donkey-riding friend used lances to attack "giants", which were really windmills.

Drum horse
Today the drum horse is used during processions, but in the past, the beating of drums and the blowing of trumpets gave men courage as they went into battle. These drums were given by King William IV of England to the Life Guards regiment of his Household Cavalry in 1830.

15-year-old, blue roan Clydesdale carrying drums and rider, from the Household Cavalry of Queen Elizabeth II of Great Britain and the Commonwealth

Into battle

The Charge of the Light Brigade was the most disastrous battle of the Crimean War (1853–1856), with huge casualties of horses and men.

Red Cross flag on World War I ambulance

The first ambulances were harnessed to a pair of horses or mules.

Whippletree to which horse's harness was hitched to vehicle

Brake

Small front wheel to allow sharp turning

Large rear wheel to carry heavy loads

Tibetan warrior

For centuries, the Tibetan cavalry used armour made of small metal plates (lamellae) laced with leather thongs. This armour, for horse and rider, was used by the nomadic warriors of central Asia. The Tibetans have preserved this armour.

Metal shaffron to protect head

Crinet to protect neck

Peytral to protect breast

Leather lace

Small metal plate

Protective crupper

Tibetan cavalry armour, used from the 17th to 19th centuries

Australian artillery

The Waler (named after New South Wales in Australia where horses were first imported 200 years ago) was the finest cavalry horse during World War I. These horses were strong and hardy, able to carry heavy loads, and had good stamina.

19th-century British cavalry spur, made of nickel silver

Sturdy stirrups

The stirrup was the most important innovation in the history of the horse in war because it enabled a heavily armed rider to stay on his horse.

War necessities

Pack horses and mules hauled essential supplies of food, water, and arms to the Front Line.

Metal barrel containing water for troops or animals

Whippletree

Tongue

World War I water wagon, made in England, used in France, hauled by two horses

Ghanaian warrior

This brass model of a warrior on horseback was cast in Ghana in West Africa during the 18th century.

The age of chivalry

From the 11th century European politics was dominated by the feudal system. Knights were feudal lords, who owned land and controlled serfs. These knights were Christians, bound by the religious and moral code of chivalry. The ideal knight was brave and courteous, and dedicated to war against non-Christians. By 1200, much of Europe was settled under feudalism and knights began the conquest of new lands. The Crusades were fought over territory, and the code of chivalry meant that leaders could depend on knights to die for the cause of winning Jerusalem from the Muslims.

Samurai warrior
This painting depicts a 12th-century Japanese samurai warrior in battle. The honourable samurai was totally loyal to his feudal lord.

European, late-19th-century brass copy of 15th-century medieval spur with rowel, which was long to reach under the horse's armour

Lambrequin, or mantling

Leather gauntlet, or glove

Blunted wooden lance

Cloth surcoat

Caparison, or decorated horse covering

Mail armour

The romance of the joust
The armed knights learned how to fight on horseback in competitive tournaments. This sport, known as "jousting" (from the Latin *juxtare*, meaning to meet together), was part of the code of chivalry. Knights tried to win points by either unhorsing their opponents or breaking their lances against the other's shields. From the dangerous hand-to-hand fighting, or mêlées, of the 12th century to the colourful pageantry of the 15th and 16th centuries, these tournaments were popular spectator sports.

Reconstruction of a pair of sporting jousters from the early 14th century

Armour fit for a king

Henry VIII of England passed laws to increase horse size by preventing breeding by small stock. As the cannon became the new weapon of choice, armour was no defence, but it was still used in royal parades.

Bronze eye-guard for protecting a horse's face, English, 1st century CE

This full horse armour (or bard), known as the "Burgundian Bard", was given by Emperor Maximilian I of Germany to Henry VIII c. 1515.

Full metal shaffron

This 16th-century Turkish shaffron (head defence for a horse) was made of gilt-copper, or "tombak". It was part of a monument to the Ottoman Empire (1200s to 1900s).

Wooden, or leather, crest in the form of a bird or animal was sometimes worn here

Metal helm

Vamplate, or metal disc, for protecting hand

Leg guard

This wooden German jousting saddle (c. 1500) was used in a "joust of peace" with blunted lances. Two bows curved round the knight's thighs to protect his limbs.

Pelham bit

Shield painted in heraldic colours, repeated on horse's caparison

Coeur de Lion

Richard the Lionheart (1157–1199) became King of England in 1189. He found fame by bravely leading the Third Crusade to Palestine.

Painful stop

Four-spiked iron caltrops were put in the ground to lame the enemy's horses as they stepped on them.

Travelling by horse

Horses, asses, and mules have transported people and goods for more than 4,000 years. The first harness and carts were made of wood, bone, and leather, until 3,500 years ago when copper and bronze were used on chariots, followed by iron 1,000 years later. Metal additions to harnesses speeded up travel times in southern Europe and Asia. But in rainy northern Europe, the pack horse remained the best mode of travel until roads were built by the Romans and built again in the Middle Ages (1100–1500 CE).

Fit for a queen
This is a replica of Queen Elizabeth I's carriage – the first carriage to be built for the British monarchy. Until then, royalty rode in carts. With steps folded up the side, the carriage's padded roof protected against rain.

Highwayman and horse
Dick Turpin (1705–1739) was a legendary English highwayman who, it has been recorded, rode to the city of York in record time on his mount Black Bess.

Bareback rider!
In 11th-century legend, Lady Godiva rode naked through Coventry.

Horse feathers
The horses of native Americans had endurance and stamina for war and hunts. Decoration was part of native American culture. Chiefs wore bright colourful feathered headdresses and adorned their horses, too.

Blinker

Blaze

Bit with a straight bar

Collar

Metal hame with twist at top as traditional Romany decoration

Breeching strap

Beast of burden
This stone frieze shows that the ancient Assyrians bred powerful mules to carry hunting gear.

The travellers
For many centuries, Romany gypsies have travelled around Europe in their caravans. No one knows where they came from, but they may be of Hindu origin.

Patron saint
St Christopher (3rd century CE) was patron saint of travellers – his feast day is 25 July.

18th-century bronze horse and rider from Nigeria in West Africa

Pilgrims' progress
Pilgrim riders featured in the *Canterbury Tales* by poet Geoffrey Chaucer.

Canvas-covered barrel top

Shaft

Sock

Nine-year-old Irish Draught horse (wearing traditional Romany harness) pulling a gypsy caravan, built in Ireland, c. 1850

Horse-drawn vehicles

Snow sled with fur-lined seats, built in the Netherlands, c. 1880

Early chariots in the ancient world had solid wooden wheels and a fixed axle that did not pivot. The invention of light, spoked wheels allowed chariots to travel faster. The four-wheeled carriage, with a swivelling axle that could turn independently, was a feature by the early Middle Ages. The poor travelled in carts and on horse buses, while the rich travelled in grand carriages harnessed to majestic horses. Care went into maintaining horses, harness, and carriages. Horses were fed and fitted with shoes, wheels were greased and repaired, and carriages were kept clean and dry.

Bronze model of horse and carriage, Eastern Han Dynasty, China, second century CE

Elegant and expensive carriage harnessed to a pair of beautiful horses

American ambush
Early European immigrants who travelled across North America by stagecoach were often attacked by mounted native Americans, armed with stolen guns.

Blinker

Collar

Terret

Crupper

Check, or driving, rein

Hame

Bit

Martingale

Girth strap

Hip strap

Trace

Tongue

Triple whippletree connecting two pairs of horses to stagecoach

Only one seat left on this overcrowded horse bus – two people will be disappointed

Driver's seat

Seating for two passengers

A type of Victorian carriage called a barouche, made in England from a French design, c. 1880

Guard-messenger riding shotgun

"Jehu", or driver

Extra luggage stowed on top

Roll-up leather curtains to let in cool air, or to keep out snow and rain

Seating inside for nine passengers

Passengers' luggage stowed in rear trunk

Way out West

Two Americans – Henry Wells (1805–1878) and William Fargo (1818–1881) – opened banking and shipping services in San Francisco in 1852, linking the Far West with the rest of the nation. The Wells Fargo stage-coaches carried passengers, money, and valuables.

Brake lever controlled by driver's foot

Two sets of reins connecting the two pairs to driver

WELLS FARGO & CO. OVERLAND STAGE

US MAIL

Step for passengers getting into stagecoach

Standing room for 12 passengers

Driver's seat

Box under driver's seat containing tools, water bucket, mail pouches, and strongboxes full of valuables

Two pairs of Welsh Cobs hauling Wells Fargo stagecoach, made in USA, late 1800s

Hunting brake, with driver's seat and space for standing room only, made in England, c. 1880

Heavy horses

In Europe and Asia, "the age of the horse" lasted from the classical times of Greece and Rome until the start of the 19th century when they were overtaken by the steam engine. Until then, the horse, mule, and donkey were the main means of transport and essential to agricultural work. They were used in forestry, harvesting, threshing on the land, and drawing water from wells. In the damp soil of northern Europe, powerful heavy horses were needed to plough and haul. Today Europe's heavy horses are exported worldwide.

Haymaking in Ireland
The horse and the donkey are still used on small farms in Ireland. Here a wagon is being loaded with hay, which is winter food for the farm animals.

Long, arched neck with thick mane

Fine head with straight profile

Belgian compact
Also called Brabant, this ancient breed of heavy draught horses from Belgium is pure-bred. They are still used on farms in the USA.

Decorated mane

Horse brass

Hame, on heavy collar

Chestnut-coloured Belgian Draught horse

Broad, deep-chested body

Before the tractor
The invention of the rigid, padded horse collar by the Chinese, c. 500 CE, spread across Asia to Europe. This impacted on agriculture, as horse-drawn ploughs became the tractors of their day. Today ploughing with horses is slower than using a tractor, but it is better for the land. Ploughing competitions take place at agricultural shows in Britain and Europe.

Strong, muscular leg

No feathering on heel of foot

Dapple-grey Percheron

Mountain climber

The Avelignese is raised in in the mountains of Italy. Used as both a draught horse and a pack horse, it measures up to 150 cm (14.3 hh/59 in).

Bridle

Collar

Saddle

Hip strap

Breech band

Loin strap

Chain trace

Chestnut-coloured Avelignese

A better brew

In about 1800, the horse became important in the brewing industry. Brewers had horses, drays, and carts, as well as a blacksmith and wheelwright. Horses were also used for grinding the malt and for driving water pumps.

Grey-coloured Boulonnais

Chestnut-coloured Suffolk Punch

French pride

The head of the Boulonnais – a native of northwest France like the Percheron – shows the influence of its Arab ancestry. This silky-coated ancient breed stands over 163 cm (16 hh/64 in).

A powerful punch

The Suffolk Punch was developed as a farm horse in Suffolk in the late 1700s. Not only does it have fantastic stamina and power, but it also needs less food than other heavy breeds. The Suffolk's coat colouring is always chestnut.

Long, powerful hindquarters

Best of France

The Percheron from northern France is the best known breed of heavy horse. Its elegance, from cross-breeding with Arab stallions, has made it a popular breed in the USA and Canada.

After the harvest is done

Every autumn horses help ready the ground for new crops after the harvest. Horses are ploughing and harrowing in this 16th-century Flemish scene.

Deep in the forest

Heavy horses have traditionally been used to haul heavy logs from forests.

Horse-drawn rake for gathering cut hay into long, smooth rows

Horse power

Without the horse, the Industrial Revolution could never have taken place. Horse transport enabled manufactured goods to be carried to ships for export abroad and enabled people to flock to cities for industrial work. Factory horses provided power to engines and machines for grinding malt or wheat, spinning cotton, or furnace blowing. Ponies went down the mines to haul loads from the coal face and also towed coal-filled barges along canals. Today machinery has replaced horses, but the term used to measure an engine's pulling power is still "horsepower".

Cog

Horse buses
The first public horse carriages in Britain started in 1564, but roads were so bad that people could not go far.

Weighing scales

COAL MERCHANT
THOMAS JEWELL

Heavily laden coal wagon, made in England, 1920

Shaft attached to grinding stones

Snowshoes
In heavy snow, surefooted horses are needed to haul logs out of forests, or sleds full of goods, like these Haflinger ponies in Bavaria in southern Germany.

Brake

Sack of coal

Lamp

Horn

Water hose

LONDON

Water bucket

Exploring the interior
Horses hauled wooden wagons laden with supplies to Australia's interior. Wagon safety depended upon the correct wheels.

Victorian fire engine, English, 1890 – wide wheels let horses turn corners without any spills

Giant iron fly-wheel attached to an iron rod, or shaft

Going round in circles
The tediousness of this circular work is all the more apparent when viewed from above.

Heavy collar

Whippletree attached to iron bar, in turn linked to shaft

Metal linked-chain trace

Long, well-muscled leg helping horse pull heavy load

Huge, flat grinding stones hidden underground

Shire horse pulling heavy horse gin, or horsewheel, inside a circular building called a roundhouse

Towing a barge
Horses and mules were often used to pull barges heavily laden with coal or farm produce along rivers and canals in Britain and Europe, right up until the 20th century.

A hard grind
This horse is being used to turn a mill wheel to grind corn into flour – just as horses, mules, and donkeys have done across Europe since Roman times. Animals were forced to walk round in a small circle for hours, pulling the rope or chain that turned the heavy grinding stone. Sometimes, a pair of horses would carry out this operation.

53

Light draught work

The common light draught horse was the mainstay of global transport until the steam engine was invented in the 1820s. Light draught horses were powerful and fast, pulling wagons, carriages, and carts. They did not belong to a particular breed but some, like the Cleveland Bay of Yorkshire, had been preserved as pure breeds since ancient times. Cleveland Bays were called "Chapman horses" because they carried the loads of travelling salesmen ("chapmen") around the countryside.

Hansom cab (c. 1850), driven by single driver and horse

Feathered plume

Crowd control
The specially-trained horses of mounted police still perform an important function in moving fast through crowds. They give their riders mobility and a good view of events.

Pack horse
For centuries, horses have carried loads on their backs, like this woodcutter's horse in Guatemala.

Pole strap attaching collar to central shaft (pole)

Royal coat of arms

Barred Victorian gaol wagon used to carry prisoners, made in England, c. 1890

Black velvet pall, or blanket, covering horse's hindquarters

Days of mourning
In olden days, a black-draped hearse, drawn by black-plumed horses, slowly carried a coffin to a funeral.

Sunday morning drive

This 19th-century print of a family outing in a horse-drawn carriage is by American lithographers Nathaniel Currier and James Ives.

Harness attached to centre pole

Pair of greys and phaeton, English, c. 1840

Regency rake about town

In English spa towns in the early 19th century, young gentlemen dashed about town in elegant sporting phaetons, driven with the top up or down.

Driver dressed in dark mourning suit

Plumes made of ostrich feathers

Coffin

Engraved glass sides

Splinter bar to which traces are attached

Pair of black Welsh Cobs, in black and silver harness, pulling funeral hearse, made in England, c. 1850

R. JORDAN & SONS

THE PADDOCK

Rubber-wheeled dairy wagon, made in England, c. 1950

North American equids

Indigenous wild horses (equids) of North America became extinct 10,000 years ago. Domestic horses arrived on the continent with Christopher Columbus in 1492. Since then horses have symbolized freedom and enterprise in North America, and increased horse numbers matched that of humans. Horses have been constant companions, pulling heavy loads in desert heat, down dark mines, and along muddy roads. The horse gave Native Americans their fastest transport.

Buffalo Bill
In 1882 rider Buffalo Bill Cody (1846–1917) held the first professional rodeo show at the Fourth of July festivities in Nebraska.

Travel today
The Amish settled in Pennsylvania, USA, in the 1700s, developing the Conestoga (a heavier version of the covered wagon) to explore the West. Their simple lifestyle sees them still using horses for work and travel.

A musical ride
The Royal Canadian Mounted Police are famous for the pageantry – red tunics and black horses – of their musical ride.

Legendary ladies
Calamity Jane, Annie Oakley, Belle Starr... the list of female legends of the Old West is endless, when cowgirls shot guns and rode horses. Bad guys, like Frank and Jesse James, and Billy the Kid, were chased by lawmen like Wyatt Earp and Wild Bill Hickok, and everyone rode a horse.

Stetson hat

Fringed leather jacket

Stock whip

Saddle horn

Flowing mane

Western curb bit

Leather chaps, or trousers

Leather stirrups

The Appaloosa with its distinctive spotted coat was a favourite mount of native Americans

Cowgirl in typical Western clothes riding 14-year-old skewbald Cob

Stampede!

Every July at the Calgary Stampede in Canada, the contests of skill and speed at this rodeo include the dramatic chuck (food) wagon races. Two pairs of horses, a cook-driver, and four outriders race to be first across the finish line.

Hollywood heroes

"There isn't a bronc that can't be rode; there isn't a cowboy that can't be thrown." The bucking horse at the rodeo symbolizes man's need to subjugate the wild and free. Wild horse races feature at the rodeo, with unbroken horses ridden to show off the cowboys' courage. Movie cowboys and their horses, such as the Lone Ranger and Silver, helped to recreate the legend of the Old West.

Buffalo hunt

American artist George Catlin painted the native Americans' horses hunting buffalo, which all but disappeared in the West due to slaughter by European immigrants.

Paul Revere's ride

Famous for his night ride from Boston on 18 April 1775 to warn the colonists of Massachusetts the British troops were coming, Paul Revere (1735–1818) and his horse are American legends.

Army roughriders

Ordinary cavalrymen (an army's mounted forces) spent hours in the saddle, so strong horses were essential. American artist Frederic Remington painted the US Cavalry in hot pursuit.

Lasso for roping cattle

Stetson

Saddle horn

Silver and tooled leather gunbelt

Western curb bit

Leather chaps

Leather stirrups

Cowboy on Palomino (part Thoroughbred, part Arab)

Sporting horses

"They rapidly flew over the plain, swiftly... whilst their manes were tossed about by the breath of the wind." This description of a chariot race comes from Homer's *Iliad* (8th century BCE). Four-horse chariot races were part of the early Olympic Games, while centuries later, the Romans raced horses in special arenas. In the 11th century, the first flat racing began in England, before riding schools teaching classical equitation started in Europe. In 1750, the first Jockey Club was founded in England. Today, competitive sports with horses are as popular as ever.

Every year in Siena, Italy, horses and riders race around the main square in the exciting *Palio*

Circus horse by French painter Georges Seurat (1859–1891)

Pommel

Cantle

Metal stirrup

A smooth leather English saddle has a very low cantle and pommel.

Legend goes that Pelops drove a four-horse chariot to found the Olympic Games in 1222 BCE.

Hard hat

Format riding jacket

Throatlash

Running martingale

Browband

Cheekpiece

Noseband

Seven-year-old dapple-grey jumper – a mix of Irish Draught and Irish Thoroughbred

Numnah

Painted wooden barrier at least 1.4 m (4.5 ft) high

Point to point
Steeplechasing began in 1752 as a crosscountry race. A church steeple was the goal, and all the hedges or gates had to be jumped to reach it.

Over they go
To jump over obstacles in their path is part of the natural behaviour of wild horses that are galloping away from a predator. But domesticated horses will only jump when directed to do so by their riders. To train a horse to be a show jumper is a long and complicated process.

In cold water

Three-day eventing tests the endurance, speed, and obedience of a horse, as well as its rider's ability. The event is broken down into dressage on the first day, followed by a cross-country/steeplechase course with a water hazard, and showjumping on the third and final day.

Fun for everyone

Mounted games, or gymkhanas, offer young riders a chance to see what they and their ponies can do at this junior level of equestrian, or horseriding, competition.

Riding side-saddle began with European royalty about 600 years ago.

Saddle horn

High cantle

Lariat

Leather stirrup

Western leather saddles had pommels (saddle horns) used by cowboys to lasso cattle.

Rein

Classic jodhpurs, or riding pants

English jumping saddle

Bridoon

Tendon boots to protect from overreach of hind feet

Girth

Metal stirrup

Anyone for polo?

Polo was invented by the Chinese about 2,500 years ago. Today, it is popular in Argentina, the USA, Australia, and Britain. Two teams of four players each hit the ball with longhandled mallets and try to score as many goals as possible. The team with the most goals wins.

They're off!

Modern flat racing – racing on a track with no obstacles – owes its existence to the Thoroughbred, first developed in Britain in the 17th and 18th centuries.

Horseplay

The close bond that has been forged over thousands of years between humans and horses cannot be broken by the rise of the motor car. The horse is popular in competitive sports, and those who cannot take part in showjumping or racing can watch it on television. Most highly bred horses must be carefully trained to maintain their fitness and optimize their chance of winning. Racehorses use their natural instincts to follow the leading horses, helped by the sting of a whip. Show jumpers and dressage horses mix training with obedience. Horses provide sport and recreation, from pony-trekking and endurance racing to international driving and classical equitation.

Away at the races
Flat racing – the "Sport of Kings" – is popular around the world with classic races like England's Derby, America's Belmont Stakes, and Australia's Melbourne Cup.

Height at withers 152 cm (15 hh/60 in)

Creek crossing
Pony-trekking is a popular recreation for both adults and children. Here children are riding ponies in single file across a shallow stream in the Victorian Alps in southeastern Australia.

Pacers and trotters
In North America, France, Russia, and Australia, the trotting, or harness, race is as popular as flat racing. The modern trotting race is similar to ancient chariot races, except that it is a single trotting horse. In pacing, legs move in lateral (same side) pairs.

Horse race
For centuries, riders raced long-distance to break the latest time and distance records, as shown in this 18th-century Japanese print.

Three-year-old bay American Standardbred driven by owner in his racing colours

Elegant dressage

Classical riding, or dressage, shows the horse at the peak of its fitness and its obedience to its rider. It peaked in popularity during the 18th century. In modern advanced dressage competitions, marks out of ten are given for excellence.

For centuries, horse's tail hair has been used to string musical instrument bows.

Hunters return

Hunting on horseback has been popular since the Assyrians, c. 2500 BCE, when prey was lions or wild oxen. Later, in Europe, as in this 16th-century Flemish calendar, the quarry was the stag, bear, or hare. By the 17th century, the English developed fox-hunting, helped by trained scent hounds.

Driving test

At horse shows, driving events are popular. In 1970, the first international horse-driving trials took place. These trials had presentation and dressage on the first day, followed by a marathon of 27 km (17 miles), and then obstacle driving on the third day.

Driving whip

Jockey cap

Shirt showing owner's racing colours

Sulky, or cart

Special harness around legs help horse maintain its lateral pacing

Horse walk

The horse has four gaits – walk, trot, canter, and gallop. Walk has four beats – left hind, left fore, right hind, and right fore legs. Trot has two beats – left hind and right fore together, right hind and left fore together. Canter has three beats – left hind, left fore, and right hind together, and finally right fore leg. Gallop has four beats, the same as the walk, before all feet come off the ground.

Useful ponies

Children who learn to ride and look after a pony develop an understanding of the rich relationships that can exist between humans and animals. In the past, the native ponies of northern Europe were used as pack animals and farm workers, and then, when a docile pony was too old to work, it was given to a child for riding lessons. At that time almost everyone could handle a horse. Today fewer people learn to ride and even fewer have a pony, but for those who do, it is a very rewarding experience.

Through all kinds of weather
Pony Express riders braved bad weather, tough terrain, and attacks by native Americans to carry the post 3,300 km (2,000 miles) across the USA in the 1860s.

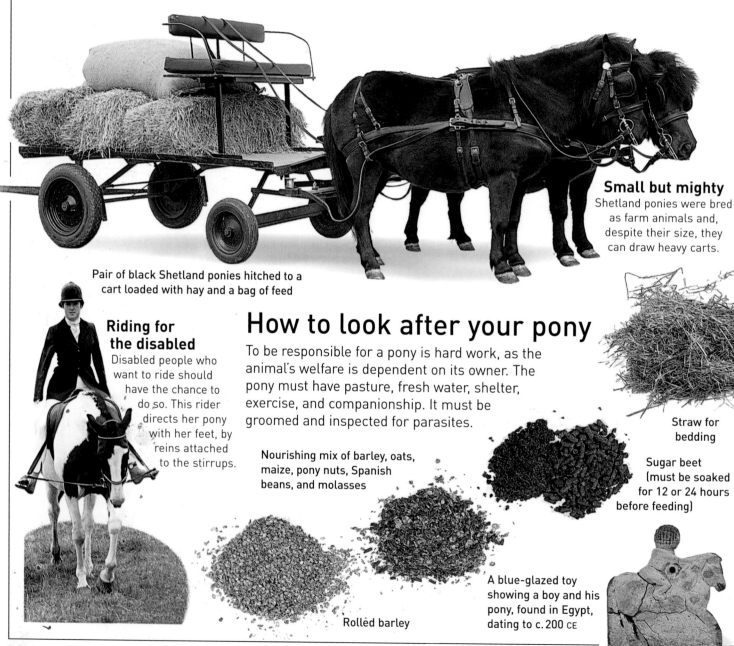

Small but mighty
Shetland ponies were bred as farm animals and, despite their size, they can draw heavy carts.

Pair of black Shetland ponies hitched to a cart loaded with hay and a bag of feed

Riding for the disabled
Disabled people who want to ride should have the chance to do so. This rider directs her pony with her feet, by reins attached to the stirrups.

How to look after your pony

To be responsible for a pony is hard work, as the animal's welfare is dependent on its owner. The pony must have pasture, fresh water, shelter, exercise, and companionship. It must be groomed and inspected for parasites.

Nourishing mix of barley, oats, maize, pony nuts, Spanish beans, and molasses

Straw for bedding

Sugar beet (must be soaked for 12 or 24 hours before feeding)

Rolled barley

A blue-glazed toy showing a boy and his pony, found in Egypt, dating to c. 200 CE

Various types of rugs or sheets are needed to keep the horse warm in winter, or protect it from flies in hot weather.

Dressage whip

Lunge whip

Headcollar for training horse to be on the lead

Around and around
Every fairground has a merry-go-round, or carousel, on which children can safely ride a brightly painted mechanical horse.

Hoof pick

Moulting brush

Hoof oil

Curry comb for removing dried mud

Soft body brush

Metal comb used when plaiting

Hay for eating

Miner's lamp

Pit ponies
Blind ponies were often taken to work down coal mines as they did not need to see their way along the tunnels. It was wet, cold, and dark, with many miners and ponies living underground for months on end.

A young boy and his blue roan Shetland pony ready for working underground in a coal mine

Three-tined fork for mucking out stables

Did you know?

The head of this herd of horses is probably a mare

A horse drinks at least 25 litres (44 pints) of water daily – about 13 times more than a person.

Within an hour of being born, a foal can stand and walk. A child takes about a year to master the same skills. This ability is essential for the foal to move on with the herd.

A herd of horses is usually led by a mare (a female horse). She decides when the herd should move on to look for fresh grazing. She uses behaviour like the bite threat to keep the herd in order.

The "horsepower" is an internationally recognized unit of the pulling power of an engine. Scientists define it as the power that is required to lift a weight of 75 kg (165 lb) over a distance of 1 m (39 in) in 1 second. A real horse is 10 to 13 times as strong as this.

People argued for years about whether a horse takes all four feet off the ground when it gallops. In 1872 photographer Eadweard Muybridge set up a line of 24 cameras and photographed a horse galloping past. The pictures proved a horse has all four feet off the ground.

A donkey carrying a load of straw

"Doing the donkey work" means doing hard, boring work. The expression comes from the fact that donkeys were bred for their stamina and endurance to carry heavy loads.

A 20-year-old horse shows its teeth

A mother horse and her foal

Horses have powerful lungs and strong hearts to help them run fast. A Thoroughbred's heart can weigh 5 kg (11 lbs), which is 16 times heavier than an adult person's heart.

The Shire Horse is the largest breed of horse, but the biggest horse ever was a Percheron called Dr Le Gear. He measured 21 hands (213 cm/84 in) high.

The expression "straight from the horse's mouth" means to hear something directly from the best source. It comes from the best way to discover the age of a horse, which is to examine its teeth. As a horse ages, its incisor teeth wear down and protrude much more.

QUESTIONS AND ANSWERS

Q Why do newborn foals look so gangly?

A When a foal is born, its legs are already 90 per cent of their adult length, whereas the rest of its body has to grow a lot. This makes it look gangly. Foals often bend their front legs to reach down to eat grass.

A newborn foal

Q Why are horses' eyes positioned on the sides of their heads?

A This eye position gives the horse good all-round vision, which is vital for spotting potential dangers.

Q Why do horses often roll on the ground?

A Rolling helps a horse to scratch places it can't otherwise reach and to shed loose hairs from its coat. Each horse leaves its individual scent on the rolling patch. These scents mix together to produce a unique "herd smell" that helps the herd to bond.

A horse rolling

Q How fast can a horse run?

A The maximum recorded speed for a galloping horse is 69 kph (43 mph). This puts the horse among the 10 fastest mammals in the world, but way behind the fastest animal, the cheetah, which tops 105 kph (65 mph).

Q Why do horses run away?

A Horses facing danger have two options – fight or flight. They nearly always run away. One horse is always on guard. If it senses danger, it alerts the others and the herd all run off.

Q When was horse racing first invented?

A The first records of a ridden race come from the ancient Greek Olympic Games in 624 BCE. It took place over about 1,200 m (1,313 yds).

Q Why do horses come in so many different shapes and sizes?

A People have created different types of horse by selective breeding. This means limiting breeding to selected animals, by cross-breeding between horse types or in-breeding within a family. This can produce a specific skill, such as strength or speed. Distinctive breeds have emerged over time.

Q How did the Przewalski's horse get its unusual name?

A The Przewalski's horse is named after the man who discovered it – Nikolay Przhevalsky. This 19th-century Russian explorer travelled around eastern central Asia. His wildlife discoveries included the wild camel and wild horse, which he found in western Mongolia in the 1870s.

Record Breakers

HIGHEST JUMP
The world record for the highest horse jump is 2.47 m (8 ft 1.25 in) by Captain Alberto Larraguibel Morales riding Huaso.

SPEED RECORD
The fastest winner of the Epsom Derby was a horse called Workforce, who completed the 2.4-km (1.5-mile) course in just 2 minutes 31.33 seconds in 2010.

BIGGEST BREED
The largest breed of horse is the Shire Horse, which stands 16.2–17.2 hands (165–175 cm/65–69 in) high.

SMALLEST BREED
The smallest breed of horse is the Falabella, which is just 7.5 hands (76 cm/30 in) high.

Shire Horse

Falabella

Identifying breeds

There are about 160 different breeds and types of horse around the world. Many were developed for specific purposes.

PONIES

Each horse's height is given in hands, next to the hand symbol.

10.5

AMERICAN SHETLAND

This pony, from the Shetland Islands, was taken to America in 1885.

Up to 13.3

HAFLINGER

The Austrian Haflinger pony is always chestnut or palomino in colour with a distinctive flaxen mane and tail.

10–12

CASPIAN

The Caspian is the most ancient horse breed, and an ancestor of the Arab horse.

13–14

FJORD PONY

This Norwegian pony is used for riding, carrying loads, and pulling ploughs. Its mane is usually cut short.

13–14.2

CONNEMARA

Fast, courageous, and good at jumping, this Irish pony is ideal for competitions.

Under 12

WELSH MOUNTAIN PONY

Thanks to its origins in the Welsh mountains, this hardy pony is able to survive on minimal rations.

RIDING HORSES

14.2–15.2

APPALOOSA

This horse has a distinctive spotted coat. It is descended from horses brought to the Americas by the Spanish conquistadors.

14.3–16

QUARTER HORSE

This was the first American breed of horse. It was used for farm work and herding cattle and made a perfect cowboy's horse.

14.2–15

ARAB

The Arab is the purest breed of horse. It comes from the Arabian peninsula, where it was in existence as early as 2500 BCE.

15.3–16

SELLE FRANÇAIS

This horse's name means "French saddle horse". It was bred for riding, and today is used for showjumping and racing.

14.2–15

BARB

This breed comes from Morocco, where it was the mount of the Berber horsemen. It is normally grey or black in colour.

16–16.2

THOROUGHBRED

This is the fastest and most valuable of all the breeds of horse. The Thoroughbred is used primarily for racing.

DRIVING HORSES

CLEVELAND BAY
16–16.2

Bred in the northeast of England, the Cleveland Bay was used to carry heavy men out hunting and to pull carriages.

FRIESIAN
15 AND OVER

This horse from the Netherlands was often used to pull funeral carriages because of its black colour.

GELDERLANDER
15.2–16.2

Bred specifically to pull carriages, this Netherlands horse is often used in carriage-driving competitions.

HACKNEY
15–15.3

The British Hackney has a high-stepping gait. It was bred to pull carriages, especially the famous Hackney Cab.

LIPIZZANER
15.1–16.2

The white Lipizzaner horse is used at the Spanish Riding School in Vienna, where it excels at displays of dressage.

STANDARDBRED
15.2

This American horse is the world's best breed for harness racing. It can cover 1.6 km (1 mile) in under two minutes.

DRAUGHT HORSES

ARDENNAIS
15–16

Originating from the Ardennes region of France and Belgium, this is the oldest of the European heavy breeds.

BELGIAN DRAUGHT
16.2–17

This horse was originally bred for farm work. It has relatively short legs, but great strength.

CLYDESDALE
16.2

The Clydesdale originates from Scotland. It was used for pulling heavy loads in cities, particularly brewers' drays.

PERCHERON
16.2–17.2

The French Percheron has been used for pulling coaches, farm work, and riding.

SHIRE HORSE
16.2–17.2

The Shire Horse, from the middle shires of England, is the largest breed of horse. It was used on farms to pull ploughs, and in cities to pull brewers' drays.

Find out more

If you would like to get more involved in the world of horses, there are lots of ways to do it. You could visit a horse show or a county show where many breeds of horse are often on display. Why not try going riding? Once you have mastered the basics, you can go pony-trekking in the countryside, or even enter a local competition yourself.

Rosettes

Rosettes are given to the winners in riding competitions. In the UK, red signifies first place, blue second, yellow third, and green fourth. Tricolour rosettes are given for championships.

Tricolour rosette

You must wear a hard hat at all times when riding

Visiting a horse show

You can see horses in sports such as showjumping, dressage, and driving events at horse shows. They range from a riding club's gymkhana or local steeplechase, to county and international shows.

Going riding

The British Horse Society produces a list of approved riding schools, so they can help you find a school in your area. The school will provide you with a hard hat, but it is a good idea to wear long trousers and a long-sleeved top to protect your skin if you fall off.

Knocking down this pole would incur four faults

Jodhpurs are more comfortable for riding than ordinary trousers

Equipment

After two or three lessons, if you decide you want to carry on riding, you could invest in some riding clothes. The first and most important things to buy are a hard hat and some riding gloves.

Pony club silver trophy

Two Camargue horses

All Camargue horses are the same grey colour. Younger animals may be darker, but their coats lighten with age.

Seeing horses in the wild

Several breeds of pony live wild in the UK – in the New Forest in Hampshire, and on Exmoor and Dartmoor in Devon and Somerset. Most ponies are owned by local breeders, but don't get too close and frighten them. Further afield, herds of wild Camargue horses live in France.

Fly fringes over the horse's ears help cut out distracting sounds

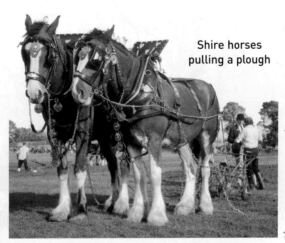

Shire horses pulling a plough

Seeing different breeds of horses

Your local county show is a good place to see horses. Many breeds are at The Equine Event, held each year in Warwickshire. Abroad, you can see Andalusian horses at Jerez in Spain, and Lipizzaners at the Spanish Riding School in Vienna.

PLACES TO VISIT

INTERNATIONAL HORSE SHOWS HELD IN THE UK

- Badminton three-day event, Gloucestershire every May
- The Windsor Horse Show, Windsor, Berkshire every June
- Royal International Horse Show, Hickstead, Surrey every July
- Burley three-day event, Lincolnshire every September
- Horse of the Year Show, Wembley, London every October
- Olympia Horse Show, London every December

NEWMARKET, CAMBRIDGESHIRE

The town of Newmarket is the centre of British horse racing. Top sights to see include:

- The National Horse Racing Museum, which tells the history of horse racing and has a collection of sporting art
- The National Stud, where many British race horses are bred. You can see stallions, mares in foal, and possibly a new-born foal - usually in April or May
- racehorses are exercised on the heath surrounding the town in the early morning

THE ROYAL MEWS, LONDON

The Royal Mews is a working stable that houses the Queen's horses and the coaches that are used on state occasions. Star exhibits include:

- the glass coach used for royal weddings
- the ornate gold state coach of 1762

THE EQUINE EVENT, STONELEIGH PARK, WARWICKSHIRE

You can see more than 30 different breeds of horse on display at this event every November. Other attractions include: displays and riding demonstrations, famous riders, and trade stands displaying all the latest products.

A racehorse being exercised on Newmarket Heath

Glossary

African wild ass

ARAB
One of the oldest breeds of horse. Arab horses originate from the Arabian peninsula, where they were bred by the Bedouin people about 3,000 years ago.

ASS
A member of the horse family. There are three types of ass – African wild ass (*Equus africanus*), and Asian wild asses (*Equus hemionus* and *Equus kiang*).

BARB
One of the earliest horse breeds. The Barb comes from North Africa, and is the mount of the Berber people.

BIT
The part of a bridle that fits in the horse's mouth. Different styles of bit include the snaffle, curb, and pelham.

BLAZE
A white marking on a horse's head.

BRAND
A mark burned on to a horse's skin to show its breed or who owns it.

BRIDLE
The headgear used to control a horse.

BRUMBY
A type of feral horse found in Australia.

BURRO
A type of feral donkey first introduced to the desert of North America by the Spaniards in the 1500s.

CANTER
A gait in which the horse's feet hit the ground in three beats.

CHIVALRY
The qualities expected of a knight in the Middle Ages, such as courage, honour, and courtesy.

COLDBLOODS
The name given to an ancient group of horses from northern Europe. Modern-day heavy or draught horses, such as the Shire Horse, Percheron, and Jutland, are descended from these horses.

Bridle

COLT
A male horse that is less than four years old and has been castrated.

CROSS-BRED
An animal produced by breeding between two horse family members, or between two horse breeds.

CRUSADES
Military expeditions by European knights in the Middle Ages to capture the Holy Land (modern-day Israel).

DOMESTICATION
Donkeys were domesticated in western Asia and Egypt about 6,000 years ago, followed by horse domestication in Asia and eastern Europe.

DONKEY
A domesticated ass, descended from the African wild ass (*Equus africanus*).

DRAUGHT HORSE
A horse used to pull heavy loads and work the land, rather than for riding.

DRESSAGE
A competition in which a rider shows a horse's skills in obedience.

EQUIDS
Members of the horse family of mammals, which includes domestic horses, wild asses, and zebras.

EQUITATION
The art of horse-riding.

FERAL
An animal that is descended from domesticated ancestors, but has returned to live in the wild.

FETLOCK
Part of a horse's leg that sticks out just above and behind the hoof. A tuft of hair often grows at the fetlock.

FILLY
A female horse under four years old.

FLAT RACING
Racing horses on a track with no jumps or other obstacles.

FORELOCK
The tuft of hair on a horse's forehead.

GALLOP
A fast gait in which the horse's feet hit the ground in four beats, and then all four feet briefly come off the ground.

GAUCHO
A cowboy from the South American pampas. Gauchos use horses to round up their cattle.

HAND
A unit of measurement used to work out a horse's height. One hand is 10.16 cm (4 in). A horse's height is measured from the ground to the top of its shoulders.

HARNESS
The equipment of straps and fittings by which a horse is fastened to a cart or other vehicle and controlled.

Dressage

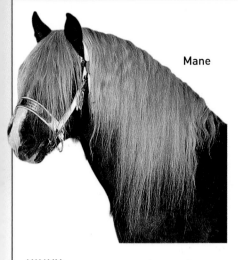

Mane

HINNY
An animal produced by interbreeding a horse and a donkey. A hinny has a horse father and a donkey mother.

HOOF
The horny part of a horse's foot.

HORSEPOWER
A unit of power used to measure an engine's pulling power. One horsepower is the power required to lift a weight of 75 kg (165 lb) a distance of 1 m (39 in) in one second and is equal to 746 watts.

HOTBLOODS
The Thoroughbred and eastern breeds of horse, like the Arab and Barb. The name comes from the hot

Thoroughbred

countries of North Africa and Arabia in which these breeds originated.

JENNY
A female donkey.

JOUST
A combat between two knights in the Middle Ages to practise fighting skills.

LIGAMENT
A band of fibrous tissue that links two bones and allows a joint to move freely.

MANE
The long hair that grows from the back of a horse's neck.

MARE
A female horse aged four or more.

MULE
An animal produced by breeding between a horse and a donkey. A mule has a donkey father and horse mother.

MUSTANG
A feral horse in North America.

MUZZLE
A horse's nose and mouth area.

ONAGER
Another name for the Asian wild ass (*Equus hemionus*).

PACE
A two-beat gait in which two legs on the same side of the horse move forward.

PACK ANIMAL
An animal used to carry loads.

PIEBALD
A horse's coat with large, irregular patches of black and white.

POINTS
External parts of a horse, such as its poll, pastern, withers, and fetlock.

PONY
A horse less than 14.2 hands (147 cm/58 in) high.

PRZEWALSKI'S HORSE
The only surviving wild horse. This horse became extinct in Mongolia in the 1960s, but is being reintroduced from herds bred in captivity.

RODEO
A competition in which North American cowboys show off their skills at horseriding and handling cattle.

SHOWJUMPING
A sport in which horses are ridden around a course, featuring fences to jump.

SIDE-SADDLE
A position in which both the rider's legs are on the left side of the saddle.

SKEWBALD
A horse coat, with large white patches on another coat colour.

SPUR
A U-shaped device fitted to a rider's boot heels, used to urge a horse forwards.

STALLION
A male horse who is four or more years old, and has not been castrated.

STEEPLECHASE
A race over fences and open ditches.

A South American spur

STIRRUPS
Two leather loops suspended from a horse's saddle with metal footrests to support the rider's feet.

STRIPE
A long, white stripe on a horse's head.

THOROUGHBRED
A horse whose ancestry can be traced back to one of three famous stallions.

TROT
A gait in which the horse's feet hit the ground in two beats.

WALK
A four-time gait in which each of the horse's legs hits the ground separately.

WARMBLOODS
Breeds of horse that are crosses between hotbloods and coldbloods.

WITHERS
The top of a horse's shoulders.

ZEBRA
A member of the horse family, found in Africa, that has a coat patterned with black and white stripes.

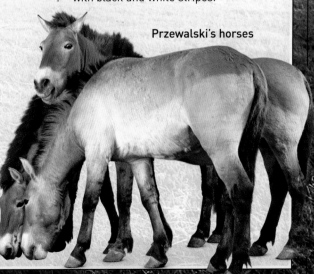

Przewalski's horses

Index

A

Alexander the Great 33, 42
American Standardbred 60
Amish 56
Anchiterium 9
Andalusian horse 34, 40–41, 69
Appaloosa horse 56, 66
Arab 38–39, 42, 51, 57, 66
armour, horse 42–45
asses 6–8, 12, 14, 16–17, 24, 30, 42, 46; African 7, 16, 22, 24; Asian 7, 16

B

Barb 38–39, 41, 66
Battle of Hastings 31
bay colour 38–40
behaviour 12–13, 40
Belgian Draught horse (Brabant) 50, 67
birth 14–15
bits 25–26, 30–31, 38–10, 45–46, 48, 54, 56–57; curb 31, 33, 45, 56–57; pelham 31; snaffle 31
Black Bess 46
bones 8–11, 21
Boulonnais horse 51
brands 23
breeds of horse 65, 66–67, 69
bridle 25–26, 30–31, 33, 38–39, 42, 51, 53
brumbies 36
burro 36

C

Camargue horses 37, 69
carriages 22, 27, 46, 48–49, 52, 54–55
carts 24, 26, 46–47, 54–55
cavalry 42–43, 57
centaur 22

Cervantes, Miguel 42
chariots 22, 26, 33, 42, 48, 58
Charlemagne 32
Chaucer, Geoffrey 47
chuck wagon race 57
circus horses 39, 58
Cleveland Bay 38, 54, 67
Clydesdale 42, 67
Cob 49, 55–56; Welsh 49, 55
Columbus, Christopher 56
conformation 40
Connemara pony 38, 66
Cortés, Hernando 34
covered wagon 35
cowboys 35, 56–57

D

Danish Warmblood 40
Dartmoor pony 62, 69
Degas, Edgar 60
donkey 7, 12, 16–17, 21–22, 24–27, 30, 42, 50, 53, 64; Irish 25; Poitou 7, 25
draught horses 38, 50–55
dressage 59–61, 68
driving events 60–61, 68
drum horse 42
Dülmen ponies 36

E

Elizabeth I 46
Elizabeth II 42
endurance racing 59–60
Eohippus 8
Equidae 6, 8, 10, 12
Equus 6, 8–9, 20–21, 24
evolution 8–9
Exmoor pony 20, 69
eyesight 12, 65

F

face markings 6, 34, 37, 40, 46, 57
Falabella 40–41, 65
farming 6–7, 50–51
farrier 28–29
Fell ponies 36, 62

feral horses 14, 20, 36–37, 57
flat racing 58–60
foals 7, 10–11, 14–15, 24, 64–65
fossils 8–9, 20
French Trotter 38
Friesian horse 41, 67

G

gaits 61
gauchos 35
Gelderlander, Dutch 35, 40, 67
gelding 12
gestation 14, 24
girth 6, 25–26, 34, 39, 48, 53
Godiva, Lady 46
gymkhanas 59
gypsy caravan 46–47

H

Haflinger ponies 38, 51–52, 66
hands (height) 7
harness 17, 22, 24, 26, 30–31, 34, 46–49, 50–55, 60
heavy horses 50–53
herds of horses 64, 65
hinnies 26–27
Hipparion 8
Hippidion 8
Homer 22, 58
hooves 6–11, 18, 24–25, 28–29, 38
horsepower 52, 64
horse sales 39
horse shows 68–69
hunting 22–23, 46, 57, 60–61
Hyracotherium 8–9

I

Icelandic pony 12
international trials 61
Irish Draught horse 47, 58
Irish Thoroughbred 58
Italian Heavy Draught horse 41

J

jack-ass 27
Jacobson's organ 13
jennet 27
jenny donkey 24, 27
jousting 44–45

K

keratin 28
khur17
kiang 16–17
Konik pony 20
kulan 7, 12, 17

L

leg markings 33, 38, 40, 47
light draught horses 54–55
Lipizzaner 31, 40, 67, 69

M

Marco Polo 32
Marengo 42
mares 12–14, 26, 64
Merychippus 8
Mesohippus 8–9
mules 12, 18, 25–27, 34, 43, 46, 50, 53
mustangs 36–37
muzzle 6–7, 15, 18, 20, 25, 40
mythical horses 7, 22–23

N

Napoleon 42
native Americans 30, 34, 46, 48, 56–57
New Forest ponies 37, 69
Nonius horse 38

O

Oldenburg 40
onager 7, 12, 16–17
Onohippidium 8
Oregon Trail 35
Orlov Trotter 38

P

pack animals 25–26, 46, 54
Palio race 58
Pamhippus 8
Pegasus 22
Percheron 50–51, 64, 67
Perissodactyla 6
piebald 36, 41
Pinto pony 37, 41
pit ponies 52, 63
Pliohippus 8
ploughing 50–51
points of the horse 6
police horses 54, 56
polo ponies 40, 59
Pony Express 62
pony-trekking 60, 68
Przewalski's horse 13, 20–21, 36, 65

Q

quagga 18–19
Quarter horse 66
Quixote, Don 42

R

racehorse 10–11, 38, 58–60
racing 60–61, 65, 69
record breakers 65
rein ring 17, 31
reins 24–26, 30–31, 33–34, 39, 42, 48–49, 59, 62
Revere, Paul 57
Richard the Lion Heart 44–45
riding clothes 68
riding schools 68
rodeo 56–57

S

saddle 30–32, 42, 45, 51; English 58; Western 56–57, 59
samurai 44
Scythian horsemen 30, 32, 34
Shetland ponies 6, 62–63

Shire horse 7, 15, 28–29, 40, 50–51, 53, 64, 65, 67, 69
shoeing 28–29, 32, 35, 48
showjumping 58–60, 68
side-saddle 30–31, 59
skeleton 10–11, 21
skewbald 36, 39, 41, 56
skull 8–11
Spanish Riding School 40, 69
sport 22, 32, 38, 44, 58–61
spurs 30, 42–44; prick 30; rowel 30
stagecoach 48–49
stallion 12–14, 26–27, 33, 38, 40
steeplechase 58–59
stirrups 30–32, 34, 40, 42–43, 56–57, 59, 62
Stubbs, George 10–11

T

tarpan 20
teeth 8–12, 18, 21, 64
Thoroughbred 38, 54, 59, 62, 66
three-day event 59
transport 32, 46–56
trotting race 58, 60

V

vehicles 34–35, 46–49, 54–55
Vikings 32

W

war 22–23, 27, 32, 42–45
Wells Fargo 49
wild horses 20–21, 36–37, 69

Z

zebras 6–8, 12, 14, 18–19; common 7, 14, 18–19; Grevys 18–19; mountain 18
zebroid 18
zedonk 19

Acknowledgements

Dorling Kindersley wish to thank:
Alan Hills, Dave Gowers, Christi Graham, Sandra Marshall, Nick Nicholls, and Barbara Winters of the British Museum, and Colin Keates of the Natural History Museum for additional special photography; Clubb Chipperfield Limited, Foxhill Stables & Carriage Repository, Suzanne Gill, Wanda Lee Jones of the Welshpool Andalusian Stud, Marwell Zoological Park, the National Shire Horse Centre, Harry Perkins, and the Whitbread Hop Farm for lending animals and vehicles for photography; The Household Cavalry for providing the rider and the drum horse, and The Knights of Arkley for the jousting sequence; The Berrriewood Stud Farm, Carol Johnson, and Plough Studios for their help in providing arenas and studios for photography; Dr Alan Gentry of the Natural History Museum, Christopher Gravett of the Royal Armouries (HM Tower of London), and Rowena Loverance of the British Museum for their research help; Kim Bryan for editorial consultancy; Céline Carez, Hannah Conduct, Liz Sephton, Christian Sévigny, Helena Spiteri and Cheryl Telfer for editorial and design assistance; Jane Parker for the index; Stewart J Wild for

proof-reading; David Ekholm–JAlbum, Sunita Gahir, Susan Reuben, Susan St Louis, Lisa Stock, and Bulent Yusuf for the clipart; Neville Graham, Sue Nicholson, and Susan St Louis for the wallchart; Andrea Mills for text editing and Hazel Beynon for proofreading.

The publisher would like to thank the following for their kind permission to reproduce their images:

Picture credits:
t=top, b=bottom, c=centre, l=left, r=right

Aerofilms: 21tl.
Allsport: 58tr Vandystadt; 59br Ben Radford.
American Museum of Natural History: 8cl, 9br.
Ardea: 14clt, 14cl, 16c, 17cr Jean-Paul Ferreo, 17bl Joanna van Grusen.
Barnaby's Picture Library: 43cr, 45bl.
Bridgeman Art Library: 41tl Archiv fur Kunst & Geschichte, Berlin; 34bl Biblioteca Nacional, Madrid; 24tr, 51cr, 60c British Library; 49tl Guildhall Library; 39cb Harrogate Museums and Art Galleries; 35t, 41tl, 56tl, 59tc Private

Collection; 57ct Smithsonian Institution, Washington, DC; 32bl Musée Condée, Chantilly; 58tl (detail) Musée d'Orsay, Paris; 60tr (detail) Louvre, Paris.
Trustees of the British Museum: 4ctr, 7br, 16tl, 17br, 22tl, 22cl, 22br, 23tr, 26c, 28c, 33tr, 33bl, 46bl.
Bruce Coleman Ltd: 12bl C Hughes; 18b J. & D. Bartlett; 39tl C. Henneghien.
Mike Dent: 23tl, 27tl, 46ctl, 50tr, 54cl, 63tr.
Dorling Kindersley: 37tr Dave King (by courtesy of the National Motor Museum, Beaulieu); 27tr, 36tl, 38 (all except 38br), 40bl, 41 (all except 41 tl, 41 br), 50c, 50–51 b, 51tr, 51c, 51cr, 56bl, 63bc Bob Langrish.
Mary Evans Picture Library: 23bl, 32tr. Robert Harding Picture Libary: 21cr, 24cb, 48tr, 51be, 56cr.
Alan Hills: 20bl.
Hirmer: 33tl.
Michael Holford: 31tc, 44tl, 47tc, 59bl, 60bl.
Hulton Picture Collection: 53b, 63bl. Kentucky Horse Park, U.S.A 67cb. Frank Lane Picture Agency: 12br. Bob Langrish: 13c, 20bl, 37tl, 40br, 41br, 54cr, 56cl, 57t, 58bc. 59tl, 59tr, 61tl, 61cb, 65br, 66–67.
Jim Lockwood, Courage Shire Horse Centre, Berks: 67bl.

The Mansell Collection: 42bl. Peter Munt, Ascot Driving Stables, Berks 67tr. Prince D'elle, Haras National De Saint Lo, France, 66bc.
Natural History Photographic Agency: 14br Patrick Fagot; 21br E. Hanumantha Rao; 36bl, 60cl A.N.T. Peter Newark's Western Americana: 34tr, 34cl, 43tl, 48cb, 55tl, 57cb, 57bl, 62t. Only Horses: 37c, 62bl.
Oxford Scientific Films: 17tc/Anup Shah/Okapia.
Planet Earth: 19br Nick Greaves.
Pegas of Kilverstone, Lady Fisher, Kilverstone Wildlife Park, Norfolk. 65br;
Spin way Bright Morning, Miss S. Hodgkins, Spinway Stud, Oxon 66tr.
Ann Ronan Picture Library: 6tr.
The Board of Trustees of Royal Armouries: 2c, 43cl, 45cc, 45cr.
Whitbread Brewery: 13cr.
Zefa: 12tr, 13tr, 24clt, 24bl, 25cr, 35br, 36cl, 46cb, 52cl, 52br.

Illustrations: John Woodcock

Wallchart:
The Trustees of the British Museum: tl

All other images © Dorling Kindersley

For further information see:
www.dkimages.com